Transition Portfolios for Students With Disabilities

To my parents, John and Mae, and my son, Anthony,
for their love and support.

MaryAnn

To my children, John, Jennifer, Patrick, and Mary for their wisdom,
humor, and patience.

Robin

Transition Portfolios for Students With Disabilities

How to Help Students, Teachers, and Families Handle New Settings

MaryAnn Demchak
Robin G. Greenfield

CORWIN PRESS, INC.
A Sage Publications Company
Thousand Oaks, California

For information:

Corwin Press, Inc.
A Sage Publications Company
2455 Teller Road
Thousand Oaks, California 91320
E-mail: www.@corwinpress.com

Sage Publications Ltd.
6 Bonhill Street
London EC2A 4PU
United Kingdom

Sage Publications India Pvt. Ltd.
M-32 Market
Greater Kailash I
New Delhi 110 048 India

Printed in the United States of America

Library of Congress Cataloging-in-Publication Data

Demchak, MaryAnn, 1957-
Transition portfolios for students with disabilities/MaryAnn Demchak, Robin G. Greenfield.
        p. cm.
Includes bibliographical references and index.
ISBN 0-7619-4583-0 (cloth)
ISBN 0-7619-4584-9 (pbk.)
    1. Students with disabilities—Education. 2. Portfolios in education.
I. Greenfield, Robin G. II. Title
LC4019 .D45 2002
371.9´043—dc21

                                    2002009349

This book is printed on acid-free paper.

02 03 04 05 10 9 8 7 6 5 4 3 2 1

Acquisitions Editor:	Robb Clouse
Editorial Assistant:	Erin Clow
Copy Editor:	Teresa Herlinger
Production Editor:	Denise Santoyo
Typesetter:	C&M Digitals (P) Ltd
Indexer:	Kathy Paparchontis
Cover Designer:	Michael Dubowe
Production Artist:	Sandy Ng

Contents

About the Authors

MaryAnn Demchak, PhD, is Professor of Special Education at the University of Nevada, Reno, where she is responsible for teaching graduate courses in the area of severe multiple disabilities. She is also currently Project Director of the Nevada Dual Sensory Impairment Project, which provides technical assistance to families and service providers of children, birth through 21 years of age, who have impairments in both vision and hearing. As part of this project, Demchak spends an extensive amount of time in homes and educational settings, assisting in meeting the educational needs of children with disabilities. She has published numerous newsletter and journal articles, training manuals, as well as book chapters. She has facilitated frequent district, state, and national training events as well as conference presentations. Demchak has previous classroom teaching experience with both students with severe multiple disabilities as well as those with mild disabilities.

Robin G. Greenfield, PhD, is Director of the Idaho Project for Children and Youth With Deaf-Blindness at the Center on Disabilities and Human Development, University of Idaho. The project provides technical assistance to teachers and families of infants, toddlers, children, and youth with combined vision and hearing impairments. Greenfield has been a classroom teacher in both general and special education. She has worked for the Idaho State Department of Education as the project coordinator of the state's VI-D Personnel Preparation Grant. She has conducted presentations at the local, state, and national level on a variety of topics pertaining to children with severe disabilities. Greenfield has been involved in the creation of a six-part video series titled, "You and Me." Five of the videos focus on the communication system, supports, and inclusion of a fourth-grade boy who is deaf-blind. The sixth video revisits the same student when he is in high school and looks at his program as he prepares for transition into the adult world. She has co-authored two manuals that accompany the video series. Greenfield is a consultant for VSA Idaho, a national organization that brings the arts to children and youth with disabilities. She has spent the past six years working with VSA and Ballet Idaho in their dance classes for preschool and elementary-age children. She has written and directed the video, "Arts Naturally: The Arts, Disability and Community," which was produced by VSA Idaho and the Idaho Council on Developmental Disabilities.

Introduction

Susie is five years old and about to leave preschool and enter kindergarten. Preschool was an enjoyable experience for Susie. She has had the same teacher for three years, and Ms. Black knows her quite well. The lively play and frequently changing activities are enjoyable to Susie, keeping her actively involved throughout each morning she is at school. She particularly likes music (e.g., opening circle with songs), art (especially when she can put her hands in "stuff" such as finger paint), and snack time. Just like her peers, Susie has favorite friends with whom she prefers to play.

By having preferences for activities and friends, Susie is similar to the other children in the preschool classroom. However, she is also different in many ways, with unique needs that will make her move to kindergarten more complex than for her friends. Susie has severe, multiple disabilities that include cognitive and motor impairments, no verbal communication skills, a hearing loss, and a visual impairment. After working with the same preschool teacher for three years, her parents are concerned about moving her to a new teacher and a new school where no one knows anything about her. Ms. Black, Susie's teacher, is also concerned about how she can pass on everything she has learned about Susie during the past three years. She is pleased with the gains Susie has made using a communication system to convey her needs and wants. Ms. Black wants to ensure that Susie is able to communicate with her peers and teachers in kindergarten without the need for them to "rediscover" effective communication strategies. She also wants to convey to the kindergarten teacher the creative strategies the team developed to include Susie in various activities. Ms. Black knows these adaptations will be invaluable to the kindergarten teacher, enhancing her ability to work well with her new student.

To help make Susie's transition proceed as smoothly as possible, Ms. Black developed a transition portfolio. She hopes the portfolio will help the kindergarten teacher get to know Susie better and that it will make developing Susie's kindergarten program that much easier. For example, Susie uses facial expressions and body movements to indicate her likes and dislikes. Unless someone has spent time with her, he or she would not necessarily know that these expressions and movements convey important messages. A transition portfolio will be vital in conveying such information to Susie's new teacher and can directly influence the success of her new school year.

WHAT IS A TRANSITION PORTFOLIO?

A transition portfolio is a strategy that documents critical information about a student. A portfolio is student specific and contains not only basic student information (e.g., age, address, parent names), but also additional components:

- Personal information
- Medical information
- Educational programming suggestions
- Ideas for adaptations and supports
- Recommendations for physical impairments
- Expressive and receptive communication strategies
- Reinforcement strategies and positive behavioral support plans
- Problem-solving techniques and team notes

Any transition can be a time of excitement, as well as one of concern, for everyone involved: students, parents, care providers, and teachers. However, for the student with disabilities, transitions present unique challenges such as those described for Susie. Unfortunately, educational transitions (e.g., preschool to kindergarten) are often planned for in haste, with only the most general information being transferred (e.g., a letter to parents after the beginning of school, transfer of the student's cumulative file) (Cox, 1999). Regrettably, the typical information provided in cumulative files (e.g., test scores, psychological report) offers little help to classroom teachers in understanding a student's accomplishments in day-to-day activities (Keefe, 1995). Transitions are likely to progress more smoothly if relevant, student-specific information can be provided to new teachers, paraeducators, and support personnel in a non-technical manner (Giangreco, Edelman, Nelson, Young, & Kiefer-O'Donnell, 1999). (Please note that "paraeducator" is used throughout this book to refer to teacher assistants and teacher aides.)

GATHERING INFORMATION FOR A TRANSITION PORTFOLIO

The information to be included in a transition portfolio can be gathered in various ways, as discussed in Chapter 1. However, we recommend gathering personal information (e.g., history, likes, dislikes, dreams) about a student through a process known as MAPS (Falvey, Forest, Pearpoint, & Rosenberg, 1997). MAPS, originally known as the McGill Action Planning System (Forest & Lusthaus, 1989), is a student-centered approach to educational planning. This approach involves gathering personal information from the student him- or herself, the parents and family members, and the student's friends. These individuals are often overlooked as valuable team members; however, they are viewed as key to the MAPS process because they know the most about the student. When other team members have the opportunity to hear from these individuals, they often learn of struggles and history they knew nothing about. The MAPS process allows everyone to gain valuable insight into the student's and family's perspectives about their history, concerns, and what is important to them in the future. Using this process leads to a solid, student-centered plan.

BENEFITS OF A TRANSITION PORTFOLIO

The transition from one school setting to another can be extremely stressful for families of students with disabilities (Rous & Hallam, 1998). A portfolio might help to ease the stresses associated with the following transitions:

- A new school (e.g., preschool to kindergarten)
- A life change (e.g., moving to a new town)
- A move within a school to a new teacher in the next grade
- A major change in educational placement (e.g., more restricted to less restricted environment)

It is especially true that educational transitions for students with special needs require advance planning if transitions are to progress smoothly for the student and educational team members (La Paro, Pianta, & Cox, 2000). The format of the portfolio is intended to facilitate collaboration among students, families, teachers, paraeducators, and support personnel. A transition portfolio facilitates the transition process and holds promise for easing the stress associated with a student moving from one school setting to another.

For example, teachers report feeling more comfortable about having a student whose disabilities include complex health care needs when a health plan (i.e., "if this happens, then you do. . .") is in place (Lowman, 1998). Presenting student information, including health care plans, in an easy-to-use manner encourages regular use by new team members as they get to know the student (Demchak & Greenfield, 2000). In addition, portfolios can reduce or eliminate the need for teachers and service providers to "reinvent" teaching strategies that have worked for the student in other educational settings (Salend, 1998).

This book describes the concept of transition portfolios and the procedures for developing them. Following a discussion of initiating the process and gathering the information to develop a portfolio, we will provide details about each potential component, listed above. Throughout the text we will offer examples from students of different ages to show the practical applications of transition portfolios. In addition, we will include "Do's and Don'ts" within each chapter that are important to remember as portfolio sections are developed. Appendices A, B, and C provide the complete portfolios for Susie, as well as two other students, to illustrate the complete process.

Gathering Information to Create a Transition Portfolio

A teacher, a parent, or any other team member who is concerned about the transition of a student from one classroom or school to another can initiate a portfolio. The idea to create a portfolio may come about for various reasons. The student may have had a different teacher, paraprofessional, or support personnel (e.g., speech-language pathologist) for several years, the student may present unique challenges, or the family may have moved a number of times. Whatever the reason, a transition portfolio can be an invaluable tool for a new team as they design the student's instructional program. This chapter will discuss how team members decide what to include in a portfolio, the different ways of collecting information, and how much time the team should expect to spend on the creation of a portfolio.

CONTENTS OF A PORTFOLIO

The contents of a portfolio will be dictated by the needs of the student. The teacher and other team members should decide what kinds of information a receiving team will need in order to design a program and begin instruction in a timely manner. A student with a mild disability who has no medical issues may only require certain educational and teaming sections to be included in the portfolio. However, a student with multiple disabilities may require a variety of sections in a portfolio. The team, including the student and the family, should make its decisions based on the student's disability and past experience. Box 1.1 consists of questions team members can ask themselves as they decide what should go into the different sections.

BOX 1.1 TEAM DECISION-MAKING QUESTIONS

❑   Is the student taking any medication?

❑   How does the student communicate?

❑   Does the student require any special adaptations and supports?

❑   Does the student have a vision loss?

❑   Does the student have a hearing loss? Does the student have special medical needs (e.g., feeding tube)?

❑   Is the team familiar with the student?

❑   Does the student need behavioral support?

❑   Does the student have specific ways to participate in educational activities?

The contents of a portfolio are personal and student centered. They should include any information that will assist a new team in understanding the unique characteristics of the student and his or her educational needs.

SOURCES OF INFORMATION

Once a decision has been made about the contents of the student's portfolio, the team needs to decide how it will collect the information. Most students enter a new school or classroom preceded by their permanent file. This file usually contains the student's standardized test scores, past Individual Education Programs (IEPs), and various consultant and medical reports. Students with disabilities may have large and disorganized files that are intimidating to teachers and other team members. The file may or may not provide team members with the kind of information they need to implement the student's program. Other sources of information may be more beneficial for the purpose of developing a portfolio and may include interviews, observations, personal experiences, and formal or informal assessments.

Interviews. Interviews may be conducted with a variety of people. The nature of the interview questions will depend on the student and the content of the portfolio. For example, the permanent file may state something about the student's vision loss, but does not provide user-friendly information about the impact of the vision loss on the student's learning. An interview with the student's family or even an eye care professional may provide clarification and information that can be included in the medical or adaptation section of a portfolio. Often, teachers do not know if a student is taking medication. Asking a series of questions of the family will help the team understand the side effects of a medication and the impact on the student's learning.

Observations. One of the most valuable ways to collect information for a portfolio is to observe the student in a variety of settings. This method can help verify a student's behavior or communication system. For example, a student who is nonverbal will have different methods of communicating than a verbal student. She might slightly raise her arm to signal a peer or she may vocalize when she does not feel well. This can be confusing for the student's communication partners and needs to be noted in a format such as a "Communication Dictionary." A teacher or other team member can observe and document the student's subtle or unique communicative behavior, and then pass on those observations to a new team via the communication section of the portfolio.

Personal Experiences. Relying on personal interactions with the student is another way of gathering information. These are not formal observations but may be day-to-day instructional or informal interactions that provide the team member with valuable insight into the student. For example, a paraprofessional who works with the student may notice that the student gets very agitated in large, open spaces. The student may begin to cry or hit people around him. This is the type of information that teachers and other school personnel need to understand so that they can prevent problems from occurring. School personnel need to be alert to a variety of information that would assist other teams and would therefore be important to include in a portfolio.

Formal and Informal Assessments. As stated earlier, the student's permanent file will provide a receiving team with standardized test scores. Sometimes these data can be useful, but it may not provide the team with more subtle information about the student. Depending on the needs of the student, an assessment may be conducted that can provide specific information for the team that they can then include in the portfolio. For example, Chapter 8 discusses the use of a functional behavior assessment that defines a particular behavior, documents where the behavior does and does not occur, formulates a theory on why the behavior happens, and then leads to developing a positive behavioral support plan. The support plan, or elements of such a plan (e.g., reinforcers), may be invaluable information to include in the student's portfolio. It may help a receiving team understand the communicative behaviors of the student and thereby assist them in designing an appropriate program.

In addition, specific team members may have their own assessments that they conduct with the student. This information may be synthesized and included in the final version of the portfolio. For example, Box 1.2 includes questions that an occupational therapist might ask parents about their son or daughter who has sensory-processing issues. The occupational

---

BOX 1.2   SENSORY PROCESSING QUESTIONNAIRE–FAMILY

1. Is your son/daughter on any medication? Dosage? Schedule?

2. What kinds of sensory input (e.g., putting toys in mouth, constant motion) does your son/daughter seek out? How often?

3. What kinds of sensory input does your son/daughter avoid?

4. Under what conditions is the student the most alert? What kinds of things "orient" him/her?

5. Under what conditions does your son/daughter seem to "shut down"?

6. Does your son/daughter's alertness state change with different activities and/or environmental stimuli (e.g., quiet versus noisy classroom)?

7. Has your son/daughter always reacted to particular sensory input in the same way?

---

therapist might pair this family assessment with a series of observations of the student. As a result of this process, certain adaptations or changes may be made to the student's daily activities. This type of information gathered from notes and assessments is important to include in the student's portfolio in an effort to assist members of the new team as they design their instruction and learn about the student.

TIMELINES FOR DEVELOPING A PORTFOLIO

Ideally, a portfolio should be developed over the course of a school year. This allows team members the luxury of gathering in-depth information about the student in a variety of ways. They can spend time with the student. They can interview family members. They can practice instructional strategies, and they can collaborate with one another to create a quality program.

But what if a team does not have a school year to complete a student's portfolio? In that case, team members must prioritize the information they think will be the most valuable for the new team to know. The special education teacher might facilitate a "mini" portfolio that consists of critical elements of a student's program. For example, if a student has medical issues, the teacher and other team members may want to synthesize what they know about the student's health and write that information up in a narrative format. They may not have the time to conduct a formal MAPS (formerly known as the McGill Action Planning System; see Chapter 2) session but can document the student's likes and dislikes in other ways. They may agree that communication is a critical area and include a communication dictionary in the portfolio that travels with the student. They may also make themselves available to problem solve with the new team as the year progresses.

It is even possible that a parent or other team member might choose to develop a portfolio over the summer when access to other members could be limited. With such a short time to work with, and given the limited access to team members, it would be very important to prioritize the information to be included in the portfolio. Obviously, information with which the family is well acquainted could be easily included (e.g., student likes and dislikes, medications, communication strategies, IEP information). Other information might need to be added after the start of the school year.

SUMMARY

A student's team can use a variety of ways to gather information for a portfolio, including interviews, observations, personal interactions, and assessments. The contents should reflect the needs of the student and act as a guide for a new team. Regardless of the time of year when it is decided a transition portfolio is needed, it is possible to develop a useful portfolio that will benefit the new team.

Collecting Personal Information About the Student

2

The personal section of the student's portfolio is a place in which to give teachers and support personnel information that is unique to the student. This information is critical to establishing a meaningful program for the student, but it may not be the kind of information found in a typical school file. For example, the student may be affected by certain sounds in the school environment and react in an aggressive manner. If school personnel are not alerted to this fact, they may interpret the student's behavior as being a discipline problem when, in fact, the student is reacting to an aversive stimuli. The student may be punished for the wrong behavior, which subsequently leads to additional problems.

The inclusion of a personal section in a transition portfolio can assist school personnel in knowing and understanding the student. This chapter will focus on the importance of gathering personal information about the student using a particular strategy called MAPS (Falvey, Forest, Pearpoint &, Rosenberg, 1997). MAPS is a planning process that asks a series of questions about a student, which helps a team plan programming and instruction.

INFORMATION-GATHERING TECHNIQUES

There are a variety of ways to gather personal information about the student. Teachers and other school personnel can look through school records and conduct observations of the student in various settings. They can also interview the student's family and former teachers. These are all useful methods of collecting information, but they are also time consuming and provide only limited knowledge about the student. For example, a file may contain standardized test scores, old IEP's, and letters from doctors regarding medical assessments, but it does not usually provide insight information about the student's likes and dislikes. An observation may provide a picture of the student in a particular setting, on a selected day, but it may not allow the observer to see the student use her entire communication system. An interview is always a helpful method of collecting information, but the interviewer may not know what questions to ask a family and may neglect to cover a wide variety of pertinent topics.

Over the past fifteen years, several effective strategies have been developed for team members to learn more about the unique characteristics of students with disabilities. These approaches have in common that they are positive and person-centered (O'Brien & O'Brien, 1998). They look at the strengths, gifts, and abilities of a person with a disability rather than focusing on the disability itself.

Using MAPS to Gather Information

The MAPS process is one such person-centered technique, originally designed to help the student's team plan instruction around general education and community environments. MAPS is meant to be flexible and therefore useful for planning in many ways. It is built on both formal and informal knowledge of the participants. For the purpose of developing a transition portfolio, the process can be specifically tailored to meet the needs of the student. It is important that the receiving team members have different kinds of information from a variety of sources so they can design a meaningful program.

Organizing a MAPS Session. MAPS is a collaborative process that brings together the important people in the student's life. These people may include the student's parents or caregivers, siblings, friends, and, of course, the focus student. Even if the student has limited communication skills, it is respectful and important to have the student present and participating, so that all may benefit from the student's perspective. Other participants may include current and former teachers, support personnel, neighbors, and peers. All of the participants bring a unique perspective to the MAPS process. Their personal experience will contribute to building a complete and detailed picture of the student.

Two people usually facilitate a MAPS session. One person acts as the host for the session, explains the process, and asks the questions. This person is the guide for the different maps. He or she may gently probe someone who is responding to a question or ask questions to clarify an answer. It is important that this person be sensitive and respectful toward each of the participants.

The second facilitator acts as the recorder of the maps. Large pieces of chart paper and markers usually are used for a MAPS session. Some recorders are creative and use colored markers to write and/or draw information about the student. When each map is completed it may be hung on the wall so that participants have a visual reference

A MAPS meeting lasts between one and two hours and uses an informal format. For example, participants may meet in the school library or lounge versus a classroom. Many MAPS sessions take place in people's homes. The group may decide they want to bring refreshments to the session to establish the time as a "conversation" about the student rather than a formal meeting. The facilitator asks each question and the participants answer in a round robin manner. If someone does not have an answer for a question, he or she may pass to the next person. The group is also encouraged to go back anytime during the meeting and add information to a particular map.

Creating Individual Student Maps. The MAPS process begins with several key questions that are posed to the participants. The answers to these questions are not meant to be long and involved. This process should create a detailed snapshot of the student and a starting point for a team to create a program. Examples of key questions include the following:

1. What is the student's background? The student or the student's family typically answers this question. Answers to this question will produce a map that highlights the student's history. For example, the student may have attended several different schools in a short period of time or had major illnesses or surgeries that have had an impact on her program. This question requires the facilitator to be sensitive to the content of what the family or the student is saying about her history. There may be opportunities to question or clarify an answer, if needed. As a guide, the facilitator's task is to help the family capture the important milestones in the student's life, but also be mindful of the time involved in answering this kind of question.

2. What is your dream for the student? This question is intended to help family, peers, and professionals think about the focus student's life as a whole and the things they want to happen for the individual. They may be dreams that look far into the future, like living an independent life, or dreams that have an impact on the student's quality of life, like staying healthy. Every person's dream for the student is recognized as valuable. The philosophy behind this part of the MAPS process is that nothing is unreasonable when you are dreaming.

3. What is your nightmare? This is an important question and one that is rarely asked of the student's family. It is also a question that is full of emotion and often brings participants to tears. Parents often talk about their fears of people taking advantage of their son or daughter or their worry over who will take care of him or her when they die. This is an important question and provides the participants with a unique glimpse into the lives of a family.

4.   Who is the student? Everyone in the MAPS session can respond to this question. The participants are asked to think of a word or two that describe the student. There are no right or wrong descriptors. The facilitator typically suggests to the participants that they use words that portray the student in a positive light. For example, if the student is hyperactive, then he or she might be described as "lively." One of the benefits of conducting a MAPS session is the opportunity to see the student from the perspective of different people. It presents a more holistic view of the individual rather than looking at the student's individual "parts" (e.g., speech, motor, behavior).

5.   What are the individual's strengths, gifts, and abilities? Participating in a MAPS session is meant to be a positive experience for both the student and the participants. The process is designed to focus on the student as a person first and on the disability second. The strengths, gifts, and abilities of an individual can include a range of behaviors. For example, it might be noted that the student can use a walker independently on the playground or sit upright without assistance. The session participants may also look at subtler behaviors like the ability of the student to "raise her hand to allow the seat buckle to be inserted." Everyone has gifts, strengths, and abilities. It is up to the MAPS participants to be creative and think about the student from a variety of perspectives.

6.   Additional questions—In addition to the foundational questions presented above, there are always maps that can be specifically designed for the student. For example, if the student is nonverbal and uses multiple methods to communicate (e.g., vocalizations, signs, gestures) it may be beneficial to include a communication map. Many students have unique communication systems, medical issues, or likes and dislikes that will be helpful for school personnel to understand as they design an instructional program for the student. The number of maps does not matter. What does matter is that the team has enough information to design an appropriate program for the student.

7.   What are the student's needs? This question focuses on what the MAPS participants view as the skills the student needs for the present and for the future. A family may list "have friends" and "a functional communication system" as priorities in the student's life. Teachers and other school personnel may look at skills such as eating, dressing, or functional academics. Depending on the student and the list of needs, the group may choose to prioritize the list so that the more critical needs are met in the current school year.

When the group participants have completed the different maps, they need to develop an action plan. The action plan should address the student's priority areas, with items added from the needs map throughout the year. The MAPS process is ongoing, and team members need to create a system to communicate with one another, as well as with the student's family, about the outcome and progress of the priority areas.

Figure 2.1 Patrick's Maps

What is Patrick's history?

- ❏ Patrick was born in Cleveland, Ohio, on July 25, 1985.
- ❏ He was born six weeks early and was delivered by C-section.
- ❏ Following his birth, he became ill and spent a month in the hospital.
- ❏ At one year, Patrick was diagnosed with a severe vision loss and cerebral palsy.
- ❏ When Patrick was two years old, the family moved to Missoula, Montana.
- ❏ Patrick began early intervention classes with the child development center in Missoula and was also involved with a regional vision consultant.
- ❏ He attended Rockland Elementary School, McKinley Junior High, and is now a sophomore at Hayward High School.
- ❏ Patrick uses a computer with a voice output to complete his schoolwork. He uses an earphone and can make choices from information that has been scanned into the computer. This is the first year Patrick has used this system.

What are your dreams for Patrick?

Mom:	To have a peer help him rather than an adult
Dad:	For people to recognize his individual strengths and not just look at his disabilities
Mike (brother):	To have a hobby
Mom:	That people understand that he is very intelligent
Patrick:	To see the Cranberries play in L.A.
Classmate:	To become as independent as he can
Physical therapist:	To become stronger and move around more independently
Paraeducator:	That he grows up and can do whatever he wants to do
Special ed teacher:	That he doesn't have to rely on people to help him
Classmate:	That he gets to go to lots of parties

What are your nightmares?

Mom:	That he gets hurt
Teacher:	That people take advantage of him
Physical therapist:	That he won't have the support he needs

(continued)

Figure 2.1 (continued)

Dad:	That people will see the disabilities first before they see the person
Classmate:	That he won't get to do what he wants
Paraeducator:	That people won't realize how talented he is

What are Patrick's strengths and abilities?

- ❑ He is very funny.
- ❑ He tolerates sitting for longer periods of time in the wheelchair.
- ❑ He can raise his body to help with dressing and bathing.
- ❑ He can feed himself.
- ❑ He is a good attention-getter.
- ❑ He has a good ear for music.
- ❑ People like him.
- ❑ He likes to learn things.

Who is Patrick?

Happy	A friend
Handsome	Part of a family
A nice person	Interesting
Brave	Intelligent
Determined	Funny
Tolerant	
A hard worker	
Helpful	

What are Patrick's likes and dislikes?

LIKES	DISLIKES
Being tickled	Hats
Sleeping on a waterbed	Bug bites
Riding horses	Brushing his teeth
Kids his own age	Loud noises
Rock music	Being alone
Animals	Chocolate
Being outside	Bright lights

What are Patrick's needs?

1) Patrick needs to have an updated functional vision exam.
2) Patrick needs to be positioned properly in all environments (classroom, lunch, etc.).
3) Patrick needs to expand his social circle.
4) Patrick needs to continue with the general education curriculum with appropriate adaptations.

Action Plan

Action	Person Responsible	Timeline
1) Call district vision specialist to arrange a functional vision assessment.	Mrs. Roberts	9/15/02
2) The physical therapist will consult with the teacher regarding Patrick's positioning requirements.	Mr. Nash, school PT	9/15/02
3) Conduct a Circle of Friends activity.	Miss Hazelton, history teacher	10/1/02
4) Interview former teacher regarding successful strategies.	Mrs. Roberts and Miss Hazelton	9/15/02

Patrick's Mapping Session

Figure 2.1 demonstrates a completed MAPS session for a young man named Patrick. Patrick is 16 years old and has moved across town to a new high school. The special education teacher, Mrs. Roberts, is interested in learning more about Patrick as she plans for the coming year. She has scheduled a MAPS meeting and has invited Patrick's parents, his brother, Mike, his former teacher, her classroom paraeducator, the district physical therapist, a history teacher, and one of Patrick's sophomore class peers.

The meeting is scheduled for one hour and will take place in the high school library. The school counselor, Miss Andrews, is familiar with the MAPS process, so she will facilitate the session. Miss Anderson, the school nurse, will act as recorder. Even though Mrs. Roberts has sent everyone an invitation to the session, she makes sure that each participant has been introduced. She also talks to the group about why she wanted them to be part of the MAPS. Miss Andrews has set up a large tablet on the library

Table 2.1 Do's and Don'ts of Conducting a MAPS Session

Do	Don't
Write down exactly what people say	Interrupt participants
Be a sensitive guide	Make leading comments
Value everyone's contribution	Place judgment on people
Be positive	Criticize people's input
Create an informal atmosphere	Hurry the process
Leave with an action plan	Forget to follow through
Make this an ongoing process	View the process as a one-time event

easel and she begins the session by asking Patrick and his parents to talk a bit about his history. She encourages them to share the things they want the group to know about Patrick as he begins the school year.

SUMMARY

A portfolio should always include personal information about the student. This information should introduce new teachers and school personnel to the unique characteristics of the individual. Using a strategy like MAPS is one way of helping teachers and support personnel get to know the student. This kind of information-gathering process is different from other more formal assessment methods because it focuses on such areas as the student's history, strengths, and interests. Having the perspective of the student's family, friends, peers, and former teachers can be very helpful, not only in getting to know the student, but also in program planning and instruction. Table 2.1 lists Dos and Don'ts to follow when conducting a MAPS session.

ADDITIONAL RESOURCES

Mount, B. (1995). *Capacity works: Finding windows for change using personal futures planning*. New York: Graphic Futures.

Bradley, V., Ashbaugh, J., & Blaney, B. (Eds.) (1994). *Creating individualized support for people with developmental disabilities*. Baltimore: Brookes

Furney, K. S., Carlson, N., Lisi, D., & Yuan, S. (1993). *Speak up for yourself and your future: A curriculum for building self-advocacy and self-determination skills*. Burlington: University of Vermont.

Including Medical Information in a Portfolio

3

Students with special health care needs represent a growing population in elementary, middle, and high schools. It is estimated that approximately 18% or 12.6 million children have special health care needs (Newacheck et al., 1998). This includes children with "chronic physical, developmental, behavioral, or emotional conditions who require health and related services of a type or amount beyond that required by children generally" (McPherson et al., 1998). This chapter will discuss what kinds of medical information to include in a portfolio. It will focus on how to develop emergency medical plans, and the importance of understanding the student's medication(s) and possible side effects. It will further discuss how to document information about the student who has a seizure disorder and other medical issues that impact his or her educational program.

COMPONENTS OF A MEDICAL SECTION

The medical section of a transition portfolio is vital for some students as their capacity to learn is often dictated by their medical state. This section should provide school personnel with user-friendly information about the student's medical needs. This portion of the portfolio is not meant to replace the expertise of medical personnel, but it can be used to document relevant information and reactions to emergency situations. Information of this kind should be accessible to all teachers, paraprofessionals, and support staff.

For example, the student may take several medications during the day, have intermittent seizures, use a feeding tube, or require a rest after lunch so he can participate in the afternoon activities. The student's teacher, the classroom paraeducator, and even peers need to know how the student reacts to a medication (e.g., gets sleepy, experiences nausea) and what to do if the student has a seizure. In addition, they need to be comfortable with the feeding routine and understand the student's energy level. All of these things will make the student, school personnel, and the student's peers feel more comfortable and secure within the school and classroom. The education team members should be aware of any changes in the student's medical routine, such as the addition of a new medication, so they can document this information in the medical section.

Teachers do not typically receive training to deliver specialized services (Sobsey & Cox, 1996) and therefore need strategies to assist them so that students are safe and their health is not put at risk. It is up to the student's team to take responsibility for documenting such strategies and designate who is responsible for monitoring and delivering health care services. A transition portfolio is designed to be personal and student centered. Each of the sections of the medical portion of the portfolio will be unique for the student. The following are some basic components that might be helpful in the medical section of a portfolio.

Emergency Medical Plans

Many of the students who will benefit from a transition portfolio will have special health care needs. The challenge for schools is to not only provide a quality education for these students but also to understand and attend to their medical issues. Developing a medical plan is one way of giving guidance to teachers and other school personnel on how to recognize an emergency and what protocol to follow (Box 3.1). The student may have several different emergency plans. Each plan should include the definition of the emergency, the student's physical changes, the specific response of school personnel, an indication of when to call a physician or the paramedics. The family or student's caregiver should provide this information. Potential causes for the emergency might be included in the plan so that staff can be on the alert for environmental hazards. The plan may also document physical conditions that are relevant to the student (e.g., Jane does not sweat) that may potentially cause teachers and support personnel to worry about the student's health. The team might choose to record past issues (e.g., seizure activity) that staff needs to be aware of during the school day, as well as possible warning signs of a serious problem.

The student's entire portfolio should be updated on an annual basis, but the medical section should be monitored and updated more regularly. The team should decide the schedule to review this section and make sure that all information provided is relevant and current.

Medication

Most children have taken medications at one time or another. However, students with disabilities may be more likely than other students to be prescribed medications due to their unique health care needs. Medications can improve a chronic medical condition, relieve pain, decrease excess muscle tone, control hyperactivity, aggression, or self-injurious behavior. However,

---

BOX 3.1 SAMPLE EMERGENCY MEDICAL PLAN

Emergency Medical Plan

Student name: Jeremy Connor   Date: September 2001

Teacher: Mrs. Craig

Definition of Emergency:

Color: Bluish around nose or mouth (Pale or red are okay but <u>never</u> blue)

Response: 1). Check for possible mucus in throat.
               2). Tell Jeremy to swallow or cough—keep encouraging him while waiting for Jeremy's 10-15-second delay in response.
               3). Stimulate startle reflex by verbal noise, whistling, clapping of hands, etc. If no response or improvement, proceed to #4 below.
               4). Begin oral suction to back of tongue and call L.P.N. If not improved after first suction attempt, call 911, R.N., and parents.

Causes for Jeremy's bluish color in the past:

- Choking
- Apnea—periods of not breathing
- Hyperventilation—periods of very shallow, rapid breathing

Seizure Disorder: Jeremy is not currently on any seizure medications. Watch for shock type jerks, prolonged rapid eye movements, and prolonged staring in a transfixed manner.
Gastrostomy Tube: If the button comes out–this is <u>not</u> an emergency–put the catheter in, call the doctor, and then get Jeremy to the doctor.
REMEMBER***Jeremy does not sweat. If he gets very warm, acts limp, and seems very drowsy, get him to a cool spot, use cold washcloths to cool him down, remove his shirt, and give him liquids!!!

---

medications may also have side effects that can negatively impact the student's alertness and ability to learn. Although not all students will have a negative reaction, it is important for school personnel to be familiar with potential medication side effects. For example, Tegretol (generic name:

BOX 3.2 SAMPLE MEDICATION RECORD

Medication Record

<u>Student name</u>: Henry Benton   <u>Date</u>: September 4, 2001

<u>Medication</u>: Metadate ER—Henry takes medication to help him attend to his schoolwork.

<u>Dosage</u>: Henry takes 60mg each morning before he goes to school.

<u>Side effects</u>: Metadate can have an effect on appetite. If Henry is not hungry at lunch, then he should not be forced to eat.

---

carbamazepine) is commonly prescribed for complex partial or tonic-clonic (grand mal) seizures. Side effects of taking Tegretol include confusion, coordination problems, speech disturbances, rash, blood abnormalities, frequent urination, loss of appetite, impaired liver function, and changes in blood pressure (Sobsey & Cox, 1996). Ritalin (generic name: methylphenidate) is often given to children to control hyperactivity and improve attention span. Side effects include loss of appetite, upset stomach, irritability, suppression of weight gain, increased heart rate, and insomnia (Batshaw, 1991).

Often teachers and other school personnel do not realize that a child is taking medication. Even if they do, they may not investigate the side effects or impact on the student's learning. The student may be punished for misbehaving or not attending to instruction when, in fact, the student is simply reacting to a drug or combination of drugs. Teachers and other team members should be aware of any medication the student is taking, even if the doses are taken at the student's home (Box 3.2). The student may have an adverse reaction to a medication taken in the morning, which then impacts part or all of the school day. Teachers and team members need to know why the student is taking the medication, the criteria for giving the medication, when to call a physician due to adverse or unusual side effects, medication changes, and effective programming that may eliminate or minimize problem behavior.

Seizure Disorders

The terms epilepsy and seizure disorder are often used interchangeably (Sobsey & Thuppal, 1996). The student may have an isolated seizure associated with a condition such as a high fever, or he or she may have repeated, unprovoked seizures, which are defined as epilepsy (Brown, 1997). There are several different kinds of seizures, which require different emergency responses. It is therefore important for the student's team members to have accurate information about the type of seizure disorder the student has (e.g., partial, complex partial, generalized tonic, clonic, tonic-clonic or absence seizures), whether a seizure of this type can be triggered by particular environmental stimuli, and how the seizure is managed. Seizure disorders have nothing to do with intellectual ability; they are a medical problem. When managing such a condition, it should be remembered that every student with a seizure disorder is an individual, and seizure management must be designed with the individual's needs in mind.

Students who have a seizure disorder can generally control it with careful medical treatment, although there are several factors that can influence the frequency and intensity of a seizure. For example, students may not take their medication on a regular basis (Brown, 1997). Some students with multiple disabilities refuse to take medication or may take only part of it, which influences the prescribed dosage. It is, therefore, important that school personnel who are administering seizure medication make sure that the student takes it in the proper dosage. They should also be aware of the school and district policies on dispensing medication. In addition, it is important for school personnel to understand that the manner in which a medication is given can affect maintenance levels. The student's family, care providers, or physician should give specific directions on how and when to dispense drugs. Mixing medication in foods is not always effective and will be absorbed in a different manner depending on if the medication is crushed, chewed, or capsules are opened before swallowing (Gumnit, 1983).

School personnel also need to be aware of environmental stimuli that may precipitate a seizure. Interviewing the student's family and carefully observing the student in a variety of environments can be helpful in determining the factors that can trigger a seizure. External events, such as stress, fatigue, metabolic changes (e.g., lowering of blood pressure as a result of missing meals), certain drugs (e.g., tranquilizers), and electrolyte imbalances (e.g., inappropriate fluid or salt intake) are a few of the factors that can initiate a seizure (Sobsey & Thuppal, 1996).

In addition, this portion of the portfolio should always include detailed information on how teachers, paraeducators, and peers should react when the student has a seizure (Box 3.3). It is important that school personnel and other students not panic, but understand what kind of seizure is occurring and how to assist the student. The student's family and/or physician can assist the school in documenting the appropriate reaction. In most cases, very little needs to be done. But for some types of seizures, intervention is required to prevent injury.

For example, the student who is having a tonic-clonic seizure (commonly called grand mal) may be injured as a result of falling on a hard surface. If the student has been sitting, it may be possible to assist him to the floor and remove any furniture or hazardous objects from the area. Nothing should ever be placed in the student's mouth during a seizure. The student may need to rest for a period of time afterward.

In contrast, an absence seizure (commonly called petit mal) is a generalized seizure without convulsions. The student will suddenly lose

---

BOX 3.3   SAMPLE SEIZURE DISORDER INFORMATION FORM

Seizure Disorder Information

<u>Student name</u>: Ellen Dater   Date: September 2, 2001

<u>Classroom teacher</u>: Mrs. Jackson

<u>Type of seizure</u>: Absence (petit-mal)

<u>Medication</u>: Zarontin (given at home morning/evening)

<u>Environmental antecedents</u>: Hyperventilation

<u>Behavioral indicators</u>: Stares out window and hums

<u>Physical changes</u>: None

<u>Staff response</u>: If Ellen is <u>sitting</u> in a chair, she will not fall. She will maintain her normal muscle tone. The seizure usually lasts approximately 30 seconds. During the seizure, Ellen will not react to verbal or tactile stimulation. She should be observed and left alone. If she seems confused at the end of the seizure, redirect her back to her work.

<u>Program Restrictions</u>:
Ellen's family does not want her to participate in activities that involve bicycles. She is able to participate in the swimming program as long as someone is with her at all times.

Table 3.1   Seizure Activity Record

Date	*Time*	*Location*	*Activity*	*Duration*	*Form*	*Response*	*Post*
9/4/01	9:35a.m.	Classroom	Math	30 sec	Absence	Observe	Confused
9/16/01	1:15p.m.	Gym	P.E.	45 sec	Absence	Observe	Confused
10/1/01	1:15p.m.	Gym	P.E.	45 sec	Absence	Observe	Sleepy

consciousness and stare into space for a brief period of time (5-30 seconds). Afterward, the student will typically resume an activity, unaware that the seizure has happened. This kind of seizure does not usually require protection strategies, unless the student is doing something like riding a bicycle that may put the student at a higher risk for injury. The team should document the kinds of restrictions appropriate to place on the student after determining the risks of various school and community activities. Also, school personnel should record data on each seizure (Table 3.1) so that they can look for patterns regarding time of day, type of seizure, physical or environmental influences, staff reaction, and behavior of the student following the seizure.

The team should also note any environmental modifications that can reduce the risk of injury to the student who has a seizure disorder. School personnel need to be aware of architectural features in the school that they may want to consider as they plan the student's day. Are the floors carpeted? Does the classroom have furniture with rounded corners? These factors will be important as the team documents the strategies and procedures for assisting the student. Some students may require the use of a helmet due to the frequency and intensity of the seizures. The team and the student, if possible, should decide the risks involved and the types of support that need to be put in place.

Allergies

Teachers and other school personnel should always be aware of the student's allergies. Some students may be allergic to certain foods (e.g., chocolate, peanuts, dairy products) and have adverse reactions to them if accidentally eaten. They can get rashes, hives, eczema, stomachaches, as well as other physical responses. It is important to ask the family if the student has diet restrictions or if school personnel should monitor the student's exposure to certain materials that might be found in the school (e.g., cleaning fluids). It is imperative that the family gives the teacher information about how to respond if a student has an allergic reaction. This information should be clearly noted in an emergency medical plan included within the portfolio.

Vision Loss

Vision is one of the two distance senses that gives students the most information about the world around them. It allows the student to interact with her environment and is critical to overall development. The student with a vision loss is not always able to develop concepts about the world around her through exploration and observation. She may not have a chance to acquire abstract ideas through incidental learning and visual cues.

Students may have varying degrees of vision loss. Some may be completely blind, while others are considered legally blind (but have residual vision) or have low vision issues. Other students may have a cortical visual impairment (CVI) where there is damage to the visual cortex or the posterior visual pathways. CVI can be the sole reason for a visual impairment or occur in conjunction with an ocular disorder such as retinal damage. Visual attention can be quite variable and be influenced by fatigue, illness, medications, seizure activity, postural insecurity, and unfamiliar environments (Crossman, 1992).

If a student has a vision loss, the portfolio should include a brief description of the diagnosis and any observations that have been conducted in the school and community (Box 3.4). If the information from prior vision reports does not assist the teacher or other team members in understanding the student's vision loss, they should ask the student's

---

BOX 3.4 SAMPLE VISION INFORMATION FORM

Vision Information

<u>Student name</u>: Paul Miner   <u>Date</u>: September 10, 2001

<u>Vision diagnosis</u>: Paul has been diagnosed with bilateral optic nerve hypoplasia. This is a congenital nonprogressive anomaly that results in decreased visual acuity, which may vary from light perception to normal acuity, varied field defects, and nystagmus (involuntary eye movements). With correction (glasses), in his right eye his acuity is 20/80 at near and 10/100 at distance. He has no light perception in his left eye. He has difficulties in peripheral vision on both sides due to esotropia (crossed eyes) of the right eye and no vision in the left eye.

<u>Observations</u>: Paul sees best in the 3- to 5-foot range. He can read 18 pt. numbers and letters at 3 to 6 inches with his glasses. He moves independently but is cautious with color changes on the floor and terrain changes on outdoor surfaces. Paul will move his head from side to side to compensate for losses on his left side and right periphery. He is taking no medication.

---

family or eye care professional to clarify additional questions (see Box 3.5). By understanding to what extent the student can see, the team will be better able to design instruction that meets his or her needs. The information in this section should be updated on an annual basis, but school personnel should be mindful that vision changes over time, and watch for any differences in behavior or schoolwork.

As always when dealing with drugs, it is important that professionals who work with the student who has a vision loss understand the impact of medication on vision. They should understand why and when the student takes a particular medication and how that medication can affect the student's learning. For example, anticonvulsants such as Tegretol can cause the student to have blurred vision, visual hallucinations, nystagmus, and other oculomotor disturbances. The student may have trouble tracking, tracing, and doing fine motor work in general.

Hearing Loss

Hearing loss and deafness affect individuals of all ages and may occur at any time from infancy through old age. The U.S. Department of Education (2000) reports that, during the 1998-99 school year, 70,813 students ages 6 to 21 (or 1.3% of all students with disabilities) received special education services under the category of "hearing impairment." However, the number of children with hearing loss and deafness is

---

BOX 3.5   VISION INFORMATION QUESTIONS FOR THE FAMILY OR EYE CARE PROFESSIONAL

Vision Questions

* Can the student wear glasses/contact lenses?

* Will the student's eye condition change?

* What is the student's tracking like?

* What can the student see when looking straight ahead?

* What can the student see on his right and left sides?

* How far in the distance can the student see?

* Is the student sensitive to light/glare?

---

undoubtedly higher, since many of these students may have other disabilities as well and may be served under other categories.

A hearing impairment is defined by the Individuals with Disabilities Education Act (IDEA) as "an impairment in hearing, whether permanent or fluctuating, that adversely affects a child's educational performance." IDEA defines deafness as "a hearing impairment that is so severe that the child is impaired in processing linguistic information through hearing, with or without amplification" (Individuals With Disabilities Education Act, 1997). It is important that the student's team understands the hearing loss. The type, degree, and configuration of the hearing loss will have a major impact on the student's ability to receive and deliver information.

There are four kinds of hearing loss. A conductive hearing loss is caused by a disease or an obstruction in the outer or middle ear (the conduction pathways for sound to reach the inner ear). It usually affects all frequencies of hearing evenly and does not result in a severe loss. A student with a conductive hearing loss is usually able to use a hearing aid well or can be helped medically or surgically.

A sensorineural hearing loss is the result of damage to the delicate sensory hair cells of the inner ear or the nerves that supply it. This kind of hearing loss can range from mild to profound. It often affects the student's ability to hear certain frequencies. Even with amplification to increase the sound level, a student with a sensorineural hearing loss may perceive distorted sounds, sometimes making the successful use of a hearing aid impossible.

A mixed hearing loss refers to a combination of conductive and sensorineural loss and signifies a problem in both the outer (or middle) and the inner ear. A central hearing loss results from damage or impairment to the nerves or nuclei of the central nervous system, either in the pathways

---

BOX 3.6   SAMPLE HEARING INFORMATION FORM

Hearing Information

<u>Student name</u>: Carolyn Hunter   <u>Date</u>: September 12, 2001

<u>Hearing diagnosis</u>: Carolyn has been diagnosed with recurring otitis media. This is an inflammation and fluid buildup in the middle ear. This fluid restricts the movement of the eardrum which can cause a hearing loss.

<u>Medical treatment</u>: Carolyn takes the antibiotic Amoxicillin twice a day when she has had the otitis media. This medication is given before lunch in the nurse's office.

<u>Observations</u>: When an ear infection is beginning, Carolyn will sometimes have a fever or tender, red ears. She may have trouble attending and following instructions. She may also be inattentive to conversations.

<u>Restrictions and precautions</u>: Carolyn may have an allergic reaction to some foods that can cause otitis media. These include: milk, wheat, sugar, and citrus. She is to avoid these foods. She is also not to swim in chlorinated pools.

---

to the brain or in the brain itself (National Information Center for Children and Youth with Disabilities, 2001).

Sound is measured by its loudness or intensity (in units called decibels, dB) and its frequency or pitch (in units called hertz, Hz). Hearing impairments can occur in one or both areas, and may exist in one or both ears. A hearing loss is generally described as slight, mild, moderate, severe, or profound depending upon how well a student can hear the intensities or frequencies associated with speech.

Hearing is critical to speech and language development, communication, and learning. There are several ways in which a hearing loss can impact a student's education. First, a hearing loss can interfere with the development of receptive and expressive language skills. A deficit in language acquisition can cause a student to fall behind in academic areas. These difficulties may lead to social isolation and poor self-concept (Konkle, 1991)

The basic information about the student's hearing loss (Box 3.6) should include specifics of the hearing diagnosis, medical treatment/medication, and any restrictions and precautions that are important for school personnel to be aware of as they plan the student's daily activities. If team members are not clear about the student's diagnosis, or if they suspect a hearing loss, they should ask the student's family or doctor. They can ask additional questions that might assist them in understanding the student's hearing loss and how it impacts his or her learning (Box 3.7).

BOX 3.7   QUESTIONS REGARDING HEARING FOR THE FAMILY OR AUDIOLOGIST

Hearing Questions

*   Does the student have a history of ear infections (otitis media)?

*   Does the student watch your face closely when you talk?

*   Does the student ask to have comments or questions repeated?

*   Does the student seem inattentive?

*   Does the student prefer to have the TV or music louder than other family members?

Table 3.2   Do's and Don'ts of Teaching Students With Medical Issues

Do	*Don't*
Interview the student's family regarding the medical status	Rely strictly on the student's file for medical information
Ask if the student is taking medication(s) and understand the side effects	Think this is strictly the responsibility of the school nurse or the family
Understand the impact of the student's medical issues on his/her education	Be inflexible
Update the student's medical section of the portfolio on a regular basis (e.g., quarterly)	Assume that the student's medical status will stay the same over the course of the school year
Communicate with the student's family	Let interpersonal issues interfere with the student's health and safety

SUMMARY

The medical section of the student's portfolio can provide critical information to team members about the student's medical status. It is important for teachers, paraeducators, and other school personnel to have the knowledge they need to create a safe and healthy atmosphere for the student. Understanding the student's medical issues and needs will assist the team in feeling comfortable with the student and therefore better prepared to provide a quality program. Table 3.2 provides important Do's and Don'ts that the team should attend to when developing the medical section of the portfolio.

ADDITIONAL RESOURCES

Agins, A. P. (1999). *Parent and educators' drug reference: A guide to common medical conditions and drugs used in school-aged children.* Cranston, RI: PRN Press.

Batshaw, M. L. (Ed.). (2001). *When your child has a disability: The complete sourcebook of daily and medical care* (Rev. ed.). Baltimore: Brookes.

Bowe, F. (2000). *Physical, sensory, and health disabilities: An introduction.* Upper Saddle, NJ: Merrill.

Kline, F. M., Silver, L. B., & Russell, S. C. (2001). *The educator's guide to medical issues in the classroom.* Baltimore: Brookes.

Krajicek, J. J., Steinke, G., Hertzberg, L. L., Anastasiow, N., & Sandall, S. (Eds.). (1997). *Handbook for the care of infants, toddlers, and young children with disabilities and chronic conditions.* Austin, TX: PRO-ED.

Porter, S., Haynie, M., Bierle, T., Caldwell, T. H., & Palfrey, J. S. (1997). *Children and youth assisted by medical technology in educational settings: Guidelines for care.* Baltimore: Brookes.

Turkington, C., & Sussman, A. E. (1992). *The encyclopedia of deafness and hearing disorders.* New York: Facts on File.

Educational Programming

4

The educational programming section of a portfolio is a guide to the student's daily program. It gives school personnel an overall sense of the student's school day by describing how the program has been designed, how instruction is delivered, and what kinds of supports are in place for the student. In addition, this section provides an opportunity to document the way the student learns best and the instructional strategies that make his or her program successful. This chapter will discuss some of the components that a team can choose to include in the educational programming section of a portfolio. It will describe how to document the decision-making process a team goes through to include the student in a general education classroom. It will also discuss the importance of using the portfolio as a place to illustrate the student's particular way of learning, as well as successful instructional strategies that have worked for a team.

EDUCATIONAL COMPONENTS OF A PORTFOLIO

The Individualized Educational Program (IEP) Summary Sheet

The Individual Education Program (IEP) is the foundation of the student's program. It is the culmination of an assessment process that describes the kinds of things the educational team (i.e., special education teacher, parent, administrator) thinks are important for the student to learn during a given school year. Unless the student's team works together and communicates well, there may be members, such as a general education teacher, who do not know what goals and objectives the student is working on. This lack of knowledge can cause confusion, particularly if the general education teacher has not taught students with disabilities in the past. The teacher may not understand why the student is in his or her classroom and how the student can benefit from instruction. It is therefore important to summarize the student's goals and objectives in layman's terms (Box 4.1). Including this information in the portfolio will assist

---

> ## BOX 4.1 SAMPLE FORM FOR SUMMARIZING THE STUDENT'S IEP OBJECTIVES
>
> ### IEP SUMMARY
>
> Student: <u>Jane Connor</u>   Year: <u>2001-2002</u>
>
> <u>Communication</u>: 1) Jane uses objects and tactile cues to receive information about her environment. She uses an object schedule to represent her daily activities and routines. Jane is working on making choices between two objects.
>
> 2) Jane uses facial expressions and gestures to communicate with others.
>
> <u>Fine motor</u>: Jane needs to practice her pincer grasp. One of the ways to do this is to pass out the weekly reader and the daily assignments.
>
> <u>Physical therapy</u>: Jane needs to increase her weight bearing by standing in a supine stander for 30 minutes a day. She can listen to the class story after lunch or do art projects with the students in the afternoon.

school personnel in deciding how to focus their instruction and interactions with the student.

Once the team members have developed the student's IEP, they need to share the summarized goals and objectives with the appropriate school personnel so they can begin the process of ensuring that the IEP is implemented effectively in various school settings.

Instructional Matrix

Use of an instructional matrix is one method of ensuring that the student's objectives are targeted in on-going classroom routines. This process involves listing the classroom schedule and the student's IEP objectives on a form (see Table 4.1) and then indicating where in the schedule objectives can be addressed. The matrix helps the team look at the interconnection of the general education classroom activities and the student's goals and objectives. It is a visual representation of when and where the student might practice the objectives she is learning. Members of the student's team should not only look at the classroom schedule but also conduct observations of different classes to understand the opportunities for instruction.

For example, Jane, a third-grade student at Roosevelt Elementary School, has severe disabilities that include limited communication skills and uses an augmentative communication device to interact with her teachers and peers. The speech/language pathologist and her special education teacher have both observed in Jane's classroom to help plan her educational program. They want to ensure that Jane has an opportunity to practice her objectives within the context of the class activities. Through their observations and discussions with the third-grade teacher, they have noted that she uses groups during math, social studies, and science.

Table 4.1 Sample Instructional Matrix

	Greet Peers	Make Choices	Use Stander	Answer Yes/No	Use Pincer Grasp	Take Turns	Use Object Calendar
Spelling M-F							
English M-F		x		x	x		x
Recess M-F	x	x		x		x	x
Math M-F		x	x	x	x	x	x
Reading M-F		x	x	x	x		x
Lunch M-F	x	x		x	x		x
P.E. M-W-F						x	x
Music T-TH	x						x
Library F		x		x		x	x
Social Studies M-W			x	x	x		x
Science M-W-F			x	x		x	x
Art T-TH		x	x	x	x	x	x

Although Jane is not always learning the same curriculum as her third-grade peers, the team decided that these group times provide her with opportunities to use and practice her communication skills. During social studies, the children are usually grouped according to topical areas. Jane is assigned to a group and uses her device to begin the period by asking the other students questions. During other times of the day (e.g., spelling), the team has decided to have Jane spend time outside the classroom, practicing skills in her school job or in other school environments.

The matrix is a valuable planning tool. Including it in the student's portfolio is a way to explain to parents and school staff how the student can be involved in a general education class and ongoing classroom activities. It is also an effective way to demonstrate to future teams how instructional decisions were made in a previous classroom or school.

BOX 4.2 CLASSROOM PARTICIPATION PLAN

CLASSROOM PARTICIPATION PLAN

Student: <u>Jennifer Dawson</u>

Basic skills objectives:

1. Communication   2. Vocabulary building   3. Hand relaxation
4. Social (group work)   5. Creativity

Activity: <u>Story writing</u>

What the class does:

1. Make one new animal out of parts from three other animals.
2. Write a story about the new animal.

Jennifer participates by using her computer to scan the animal choices. She will choose three animals. She will then scan details about each character and story (e.g., boy or girl, day or night, etc.).

<u>Assistance from peers/paraeducator</u>: Help Jennifer put her name on her paper.

<u>Materials needed</u>: Computer, peers, paper, and pencil

Classroom Participation Plans

Once a decision has been made to place the student in a particular setting, it is important to document how the student will participate in classroom activities. A classroom participation plan (Gee, Alwell, Graham, & Goetz, 1994) describes (a) an activity that is planned for the class, (b) what the goal is for the class, and (c) how the activity is adapted for the student. The plan (Box 4.2) also specifies materials that will be needed to help the student participate in the class, instructional cues for the teacher, peers, or paraeducator, and the IEP objectives to be addressed within the activity. Team members can organize classroom participation plans by subject area and maintain them in the portfolio or in a separate binder. The plans can be added to, expanded upon, and changed depending on the activity and upcoming grade level or subject area. A series of completed participation plans can assist the student's new team in understanding how the student participates in activities, as well as provide ideas for future classes.

Successful Instructional Strategies

Another key component of a portfolio's educational section is information about instructional strategies. Depending upon the student, this section may include information about learning styles, environmental influences, physical factors, and instructional cues that work for the student during an instructional period.

Learning Style. We all have our own way of learning. Students with disabilities also learn and take in information in a variety of ways. As with anyone, they will use their strengths. For example, if they have a visual or auditory loss, they may rely more on tactile and/or kinesthetic ways of receiving information. Or, if they have a vision impairment, they may use their auditory channel more. It is important for school personnel to talk to parents about how they think their son or daughter learns best. The student's teacher or other school personnel should also observe the student in a variety of settings to determine how the student learns. Does he use his vision sometimes and not others? Does he seek out certain kinds of input? Do the people who interact with the student understand how he learns? What kinds of information do they need to accommodate and teach the student?

Physical Influences. As teachers and paraeducators prepare for instruction, they should be aware of the student's physical state and how it influences instruction. If the student uses a wheelchair, the instructor needs to make sure that she is positioned correctly in the chair so she is comfortable and able to use her vision. Other things to document in this section might include what time of day the student appears to learn best (e.g., morning versus afternoon), or cues that affect the student's alertness state (e.g., starting the activity with a few minutes of proprioceptive input like deep hand massage). Although the student's medication(s) should be listed in the medical section of the portfolio this educational programming section is another place to note the reactions the student might have from taking a medication. It is important to understand the potential side effects of medications and the impact they can have on the student's alertness state and learning.

Environmental Factors. Part of creating a setting that is conducive to learning is making sure that the environment is structured to accommodate the learner. The student's team members should make sure they understand what kind of environmental factors influence the student's learning. Does the student have a visual impairment and therefore need to be sitting where there is no glare? Does noise affect the student's concentration? Does the student have a "better side" for vision or hearing? Does the person who is interacting with the student (e.g., teacher, paraeducator, peer) need to be positioned in a certain way so the student can see him or her? All of these questions are important to answer in order to accommodate the student and create a quality learning environment.

Answers to these and other environmental questions can be had by observing the student in a particular setting, interviewing previous and present school staff, and talking to the student's family or caregiver. The instructional section of the portfolio is the place to document these subtleties, which can potentially have a great impact on the student's program.

Instructional Scripted Routines

There are many things that a new team needs to know about the student with a disability. For example, the student may require a set

Table 4.2 Sample Scripted Routine

Touch cue (How you give Mary nonverbal information)	Verbal (What you say to Mary)	Pause (Wait for 10 seconds and look for response)	Action (What you do after Mary responds or pause is over)
1. Undo buttons on Mary's sweater.	"It's time to take your sweater off."	PAUSE OBSERVE	Continue to step 2.
2. Rub Mary's arm.	"Time to take your sweater off."	PAUSE OBSERVE	Continue to step 3.
3. Gently tug at arm of sweater.	"Take your arm out of the sweater."	PAUSE OBSERVE	Remove arm from sleeve.
4. Pat other arm.	"Take this arm out."	PAUSE OBSERVE	Remove arm from other sleeve.

routine and consistency throughout the day or she may become aggressive. She may need to be given instruction in a systematic manner that requires teachers and paraprofessionals to understand specific instructional techniques (e.g., verbal instructions, touch cues, pausing strategies, and reinforcement). Using a scripted routine (Mirenda & Hunt, 1990) is another way to assist school personnel in creating meaningful instructional opportunities for the student who has trouble processing verbal input. Scripted routines (Table 4.2) require school personnel to understand the types of communication, both verbal and nonverbal, that will allow the student to participate in and respond to an instructional interaction. Developing a series of scripted routines can remind teachers, paraeducators, and peers to use language and physical prompts that are specific to the activity.

A scripted routine is composed of four steps. The first step involves a "touch cue" that gives the student information in addition to any spoken words. This cue should be the same each time the activity takes place, and all support people who work with the student on the particular activity should use the same language. The second step consists of the "verbal" instructions that are spoken while giving the touch cue. The words don't have to be exact but should be natural and follow the spirit of the written script. The third step, and something that is often forgotten, is "pausing" after the touch/verbal cue. Many students with disabilities require additional time to process information, and the use of pausing can be a very effective strategy in eliciting a response. The instructor should pause at least 10 seconds when waiting for a response from the student. A "response" is any motor movement or vocalization that appears to be deliberate or that can be interpreted as being deliberate. During a pause, the instructor should watch the student's face and head while keeping his or her hand on a body part (e.g., arm, leg). The instructor will then be able to notice and react to any physical response the student makes. If the

Table 4.3 Educational Do's and Don'ts

Do	*Don't*
Take the time to observe the student in a variety of settings	Assume the student can't participate in an activity
Be consistent	Answer for the student
Practice pausing	Use inappropriate cues
Focus on the student's strengths/abilities	Hurry through a teaching routine

student does not respond after 10 seconds, the instructor should repeat the touch/verbal cue and wait another 10 seconds. If the student still does not respond, the instructor should tell the student he or she will "help" them and continue with the routine.

The final step of a scripted routine is the "action" taken by the instructor (e.g., helping the student dress/undress for swimming) once the student has responded to the touch/verbal cues and the pause. The instructor should also talk to the student when he or she responds (e.g., "Oh, you moved your foot; I will put on your sock."). The student needs to know that the instructor noticed what he or she did and that something will happen as a result of their communication.

Developing a series of scripted routines is one way of providing instructional consistency in the student's school program. This strategy can provide valuable information to new teachers and paraeducators about the prompts that will help the student be a successful learner. Including multiple scripts in the student's transition portfolio gives new teachers and support personnel a mini-inservice training in direct instruction as well as the student's communication system.

SUMMARY

The educational programming section is a key component of the student's transition portfolio. It can assist new teachers in understanding the student's educational focus and how skills can be practiced in a variety of environments. Table 4.3 addresses important Dos and Don'ts that should be attended to when developing this section of the portfolio. This section is also a place to document the unique learning characteristics of the student. This information can save new teachers and other team members valuable time in designing and implementing instructional programs.

ADDITIONAL RESOURCES

Cavallaro, C. C., & Haney, M. (1999). *Preschool inclusion*. Baltimore: Brookes.

Doyle, M. B. (2002). *The paraprofessional's guide to the inclusive classroom: Working as a team* (2nd ed.). Baltimore: Brookes.

Hannaford, C. (1995). *Smart moves: Why learning is not all in your head.* Arlington, VA: Great Ocean Publishers.

Janney, R., & Snell, M. E. (2000). *Teacher's guides to inclusive practices: Modifying school work.* Baltimore: Brookes.

Koegel, R. L., & Koegel, L. K. (Eds.). (1995). *Teaching children with autism: Strategies for initiating positive interactions and improving learning opportunities.* Baltimore: Brookes.

Torres, I., & Corn, A. L. (1990). *When you have a visually handicapped child in your classroom: Suggestions for teachers.* New York: American Foundation for the Blind.

Adaptations and Supports

5

Regardless of educational placement, the student with a disability will typically benefit from a variety of adaptations and supports: assistive technology; individualized modifications to instruction, environment, or materials; or support or assistance from other people. In addition, some disabilities (e.g., vision and hearing) require specialized accommodations. The needs of the student determine the particular adaptations and supports to be provided. This chapter will focus on individualized adaptations specific to a particular student rather than whole class modifications (e.g., cooperative groups, multilevel teaching) that are designed to benefit all students, whether they have disabilities or not.

The portfolio should delineate the specific type of adaptations needed and the activities in which they are likely to be used by the student. This information can be included in the portfolio in various ways: (a) a general form listing all potential adaptations needed by the student; (b) separate forms, by class or activity, listing potential adaptations for that class or activity; or (c) a form or letter directly from the student to each teacher, specifying the adaptations needed in that particular class. Having the student complete a form or write a brief letter to a teacher can be an especially beneficial strategy as the student gets older and should begin to self-advocate.

ASSISTIVE TECHNOLOGY

Assistive technology (AT) devices are defined within the Individuals With Disabilities Education Act as "any item, piece of equipment, or product system, whether acquired commercially off the shelf, modified, or customized, that is used to increase, maintain, or improve functional capabilities of a child with a disability." AT devices can range from no or low technology (e.g., pencil grips, special paper, simple switches) to high technology (e.g., laptop computers, sophisticated communication devices). AT can be used to facilitate student independence in a wide variety of academic and nonacademic areas: writing, reading, mathematics, studying, communicating, engaging in recreational activities, and performing activities of daily living. In addition, specialized AT devices are available for the student who has physical impairments (see Chapter 6 for a discussion of supported sitting devices) as well as the student who has vision and/or hearing impairments.

It is important to remember that AT recommendations are made on a student-by-student basis. Even students who have the same disability can have very different AT needs. In addition, when deciding whether or not AT is needed, the skills or abilities required by the AT device must be taken into consideration. For example, some computer software aimed at assisting students in written communication requires typing skills and at least fourth-grade reading and writing skills. For some students with disabilities, this type of software would be too difficult and other recommendations would be more appropriate.

Once an educational team has gathered assessment information and determined what needs can be met through assistive technology, then those recommendations and their implementation need to be documented. This documentation should be included in the student's portfolio. The form in Figure 5.1 can be used to detail the AT being used by the student.

INDIVIDUALIZED ACCOMMODATIONS TO INSTRUCTION, ENVIRONMENT, OR MATERIALS

A wide range of modifications and adaptations can be made to allow all students who have disabilities, mild to severe, to access the curriculum. Some of these accommodations may be very simple, while others may be more complex. In addition, some students will require numerous accommodations to be put into place, while other students will need relatively few. The following categories will highlight a few types of modifications and accommodations that are possible.

Instructional Accommodations

Minor modifications to the style of instruction are sometimes all that the student may require. In other cases, the student may also need to complete assignments or tests in an alternate manner. Such adaptations allow the student with disabilities to access information or to have learning evaluated. See the listing of potential instructional accommodations in Figure 5.2. Please note that this listing is not all-inclusive.

Environmental Accommodations

Some students will require a change to the physical environment in order for them to access information. As is the case in the other areas of potential modifications, some environmental modifications are simple while

Figure 5.1 Assistive Technology Checklist

Student:_____   Class:_____

Communication:

____Communication board or
      book (objects, line drawings,
      photos)
____Simple voice output device
____Voice output device with
      levels
____Voice output device with
      dynamic display
____Other:_____
_____

Writing:

____Adaptive pen/pencil grips
____Special pens (e.g., bold, black-
      pens; weighted pens, ring-pens)
____Special paper (e.g., bold lines,
      raised lines)
____Writing guides (e.g., check
      guide, signature guide)
____Slant board
____Spell checker
____Talking dictionary or
      thesaurus
____Computer software:
_____
_____
____Computer keyguard
____Alternate keyboard
____Alternate mouse or track ball
____Other:_____
_____

Mathematics:

____Calculator (e.g., large keys,
      voice output, printout)
____Adapted clocks and watches
      (e.g., large numbers, lighted,
      voice output)
____Special measuring tools
____Talking thermometer
____Abacus
____Number line
____Computer software:
_____
_____

Reading:

____Books on tape
____Computer software:
_____
_____

Organizational and study skills:

____Schedules and calendars as
      organizers
____Highlighters, highlight tape, etc.
____Colored file folders to
      organize materials
____Tactile materials (e.g., maps)
____Computer software:
_____
_____

Recreation activities:

____Switches
____Battery adapters
____Adapted playing cards (e.g.,
      large numbers, card holder,
      automatic shuffler)
____Adapted games (e.g., large print,
      textures)
____Adapted balls (e.g., with
      noisemakers, tactile)
____Adapted toys (e.g., handles,
      textures, for use with switches)
____Computer software:
_____
_____

Activities of daily living:

____Adapted drinking cups
____Adapted eating utensils
____Adapted plates and bowls
____Non-slip placemats
____Self-dressing aids (e.g., button
      hooks, zipper pulls, spyrolaces)
____Reaching devices
____Large button telephone
____Talking caller ID

Comments:

Figure 5.2   Checklist of Necessary Instructional, Environmental, and Material Accommodations

Student:_____   Class:_____

INSTRUCTIONAL MODIFICATIONS

In-class instruction:

_____Introduce new materials using advance organizers
_____Provide an outline of the lecture
_____Highlight key words or new terms
_____Provide concrete examples of abstract concepts
_____Provide lecture notes
_____Allow audiotapes of lectures
_____Allow student to copy another student's notes
_____Provide student with copies of overhead transparencies
_____Other:_____

Providing instructions:

_____Provide oral instructions clearly and concisely
_____Repeat oral instructions
_____Ask the student to repeat back instructions
_____Provide instructions in writing
_____Provide a demonstration of what is to be done
_____Other:_____

Independent work assignments:

_____Decrease number of items to be completed
_____Allow all work to be completed in print (i.e., no cursive)
_____Allow written assignments to be completed on the computer
_____Allow additional time
_____Other:_____

Alternative student responses:

_____Allow oral responses from student
_____Have student tape responses
_____Allow drawings instead of written responses
_____Ask yes/no questions for comprehension checks
_____Other:_____

Tests and evaluation of student learning:

_____Provide a practice test
_____Extended time
_____Oral exams with oral responses
_____Provide an alternative test (e.g., multiple choice instead of essay)
_____Provide an answer list for fill-in-the-blank exams
_____Dictation of answers for essay exams
_____Answer questions directly on the exam
_____Disregard spelling and grammatical errors
_____Allow use of dictionary, spell checker, or calculator
_____Allow submission of alternative assignments
_____Other:_____

Environmental Modifications

_____Preferential seating (e.g., near teacher, near a focused student)
_____Quiet area for study
_____Study carrel for independent work
_____A private location for the student to take a break
_____Minimize auditory distractions
_____Minimize visual distractions
_____Modify lighting
_____More physical space for the student to maneuver
_____Other:_____

MODIFICATIONS TO MATERIALS

Using handouts and visual aids:

_____Use clear copies
_____Provide copies on colored paper for some students
_____Use large print
_____Provide a limited amount of information per handout or visual aid
_____Darken items difficult to read or see
_____Other:_____

Independent work assignments:

_____Intersperse practice items with new material
_____Provide copies of textbook or workbook pages that can be written on
_____Provide examples of correct responses
_____Highlight key parts of directions
_____Use color cues for starting and ending points
_____Provide enough space for answers
_____Allow student to supplement written answers with pictures or drawings
_____Other:_____

Reading:

_____Books on tape
_____Written material paired with photos, pictures, or objects
_____Use of highlighting tape
_____Use of colored transparencies
_____Other:_____

Comments:

others are more involved. For example, a student may need preferential seating for any number of reasons (vision impairment, hearing impairment, attention difficulties), and this is relatively easy to accomplish. Other environmental modifications may require more creative planning (e.g., finding a private location, still with some supervision, for a student to take a break). See Figure 5.2 for potential environmental modifications.

Modifications to Materials

In some cases, actually making changes to the instructional materials will make it easier for the student to learn. These material modifications may be relatively minor (e.g., use of highlighting tape) and in other cases will require advanced planning (e.g., obtaining books on tape). There are some simple materials that a teacher can keep on hand in the classroom to make minor material modifications quickly: different colored Post-it notes, blank white labels, black felt tip marker, colored markers or high-lighters, batteries for switch-activated devices, colored pictures grouped by category, and glue sticks for adding pictures to reports (Downing & Demchak, 2002). Figure 5.2 includes a listing of potential modifications to materials.

Summary of Accommodations

It is important to note that accommodations are identified according to student need, through the IEP process, and included in the IEP. Students with disabilities often benefit from multiple accommodations from the three categories discussed earlier. It is helpful to list these accommodations on one form, which could then be shared with relevant team members. This form could be a checklist (see Figure 5.2) or in a form coming from the student (see Figure 5.3).

SPECIALIZED ACCOMMODATIONS FOR VISUAL AND HEARING IMPAIRMENTS

Vision and hearing are the two main senses students use to learn. Thus, if the student has any degree of impairment in either of these areas, it is extremely important that accommodations be documented to maximize student learning. In both areas, the type of impairment as well as the degree of loss will impact the recommended accommodations.

Visual Impairments

Recommendations to address impairments in vision will depend upon factors such as the student's visual acuity (i.e., how well the student sees from specified distances), stability of the student's eye condition, and how well vision is used by the student. A key member of the educational team

Figure 5.3 Student Form Specifying Needed Accommodations

IEP ACCOMMODATIONS

For _____

This form specifies that the following accommodations are included within the IEP for _____.

Our signatures below indicate that we have received a copy of this form and understand that these accommodations are included in the IEP.

_____   _____ _____ _____

Student Signature   Date   Special Ed. Teacher   Date

_____   _____ _____ _____

General Ed. Teacher   Date   Other   Date

for the student who has visual impairments is a vision specialist. The specialist might suggest adaptations in several areas including mobility, position of the student in the classroom, color and contrast, lighting, spacing and arranging of materials, enlarging print, as well as use of magnification devices. Cox and Dykes (2001) provide detailed checklists that can be used to document (1) adaptations for outdoor and indoor orientation and mobility and (2) adaptations for classroom strategies. There are also AT recommendations that might be appropriate for the student with a visual impairment (e.g., computer screen magnifiers, closed circuit television, a screen reader, Braille translation software). AT recommendations and other adaptations are aimed at helping the student with visual impairments to most effectively and efficiently use any residual vision to maximize learning. As in other areas of potential accommodations, it is likely that the student with visual impairments will use more than one. Documenting these adaptations for inclusion in the portfolio can be done using the form in Figure 5.3.

Hearing Impairments

Likewise, if the student has a hearing impairment, it would be extremely beneficial for the educational team to include someone, such as a teacher of students with hearing impairments or an audiologist, who is knowledgeable about the specialized accommodations needed. It will likely be necessary to modify instructional strategies as well as the physical environment. Many of the potential adaptations listed in Figure 5.2 would also be beneficial for this student (e.g., preferential seating, minimizing auditory distractions). In addition, there are a variety of recommendations that are specific to hearing impairments:

- Speak at normal levels at a close range (e.g., not from across the room).
- Face directly toward the student.
- Keep mouth free of obstructions (e.g., hands in front of mouth).
- Use exaggerated tone and pitch to help the student identify that a question is being asked or a command given.
- Use additional cues (e.g., tapping) to draw student's attention to materials.
- Draw the student's attention to environmental sounds (e.g., bells ringing, doors slamming) (Downing & Demchak, 2002).

Additional specialized accommodations might also be needed. For example, the student might need a sign language interpreter and/or might use an assistive listening device (e.g., hearing aids, FM systems). Recommendations specific to hearing impairments and specialized accommodations could be included on the form in Figure 5.3.

ASSISTANCE FROM OTHER PEOPLE

In some situations, the team will decide that the adaptation needed is in the form of assistance from another person. This assistance might come from peers, volunteers, or paid paraeducators. Due to school district constraints (e.g., finite financial resources), as well as to foster student independence (e.g., students becoming too dependent upon paid paraeducators), a recommended practice is to use natural supports available within the school setting whenever possible (Demchak, 1997). Natural supports within the school setting include same-age peer partnering, cross-age peer partnering (e.g., fourth graders supporting first graders), parent volunteers, high school students acting as teacher assistants to earn school credit or service learning hours, and university or college practicum students. However, sometimes

Table 5.1 Providing the Student With Assistance From Natural or Paid
Supports

Do	Don't
Use natural supports whenever possible before moving to paid supports	Use paid supports unless truly necessary
Allow the student with a disability to provide assistance to others	Have the student with a disability always at the "receiving" end of support relationships
Encourage paraeducators to assist all students in the classroom	Have the paraeducator focus exclusively on the student with a disability
Provide training to all individuals providing support to the student with a disability	Expect natural or paid supports to know what to do without being trained
Provide supervision on a regular basis to both natural and paid supports	Allow those providing supports to interact with the student without regular supervision
Provide feedback, on a regular basis, to all individuals who are providing support to the student with a disability	Allow those providing supports to continue without being given feedback on how they are performing
Remember the teacher must continue to have "hands-on" experiences with the student with a disability	Hand over all teaching responsibilities to those providing assistance

paid paraeducator support will be deemed necessary to meet the student's educational needs. Regardless of whether natural or paid supports are being used, all individuals providing support will need to be trained so that supports are appropriately provided to the student with a disability. Table 5.1 suggests Do's and Don'ts regarding the provision of personal support for the student. As was the case with accommodations, specific recommendations regarding the use of natural supports or paid supports can be incorporated into the form in Figure 5.3.

SUMMARY

The student with a disability will likely require a variety of adaptations and supports to maximize learning. These can range from the extensive use of complex technology to simpler modifications made to the environment or to instruction to the use of support people. Regardless of the complexity of the adaptations and supports provided, it is important to remember that all are individualized and determined by the student's educational need. The portfolio provides key means of documenting how the student's needs are being met.

ADDITIONAL RESOURCES

Blazer, B. (1999). Developing 504 classroom accommodation plans: A collaborative, systematic parent-student-teacher approach. *TEACHING Exceptional Children, 32*(2), 28-33.

Flexer, C. (1999). *Facilitating hearing and listening in young children* (2nd ed.). San Diego, CA: Singular.

Hoover, J. J., & Patton, J. R. (1997). *Curriculum adaptations for students with learning and behavior problems: Principles and practices.* Austin, TX: PRO-ED.

Levack, N. (1991). *Low vision: A resource guide with adaptations for students with vision impairments* (2nd ed.). Austin: Texas School for the Blind and Visually Impaired.

Luckner, J., Bowen, S., & Carter, K. (2001). Visual teaching strategies for students who are deaf or hard of hearing. *TEACHING Exceptional Children, 33*(3), 38-44.

Schloss, P. J., Smith, M. A., & Schloss, C. N. (2001). *Instructional methods for secondary students with learning and behavior problems* (3rd ed.). Boston: Allyn & Bacon.

Special Considerations for Students With Physical Impairments

6

Students with physical impairments typically are limited in how they can move as well as in how they can manipulate items. Thus, it is important for the educational team to implement strategies that will assist these students in dealing with these physical limitations. The types of accommodations especially relevant to students with physical impairments include (a) positioning students appropriately to participate in activities, (b) using assistive technology, and (c) using communication devices (Downing & Demchak, 2002). This chapter will focus on positioning students appropriately since assistive technology is covered in Chapter 5 and communication devices are addressed in Chapter 7. This chapter will specifically concentrate on information related to positioning that should be included in a portfolio.

Physical therapists (PT) and occupational therapists (OT) play essential roles in developing this portion of the portfolio. First, PTs and OTs should collaborate regarding the information to be included in the portfolio. Second, they should provide student-specific training to team members prior to the educational team implementing the directions indicated in the portfolio.

APPROPRIATE POSITIONING OF STUDENTS WITH PHYSICAL IMPAIRMENTS

In order for students with physical impairments to participate in ongoing classroom activities in a meaningful way, it is necessary to ensure that they are appropriately positioned physically. Appropriate positioning can be either static (e.g., using positioning equipment) or dynamic (e.g., positions obtained through therapeutic handling) (Rainforth & York-Barr, 1996). Both approaches are aimed at placing the student in a way that normalizes muscle tone while maintaining aligned body posture (Rainforth & York-Barr, 1996).

Using Positioning Equipment

All individuals, with and without disabilities, require numerous position changes throughout the day. Individuals without disabilities are almost constantly adjusting their positions. However, students with physical disabilities often need someone to help them change position or require specific equipment to assist them in being stable. In a school setting, the type of adaptive equipment used will vary depending on the student's needs as well as the activities in which the student will be participating. PTs and OTs will make recommendations regarding what equipment is appropriate for a particular student. It is likely that one student will be using more than one piece of positioning equipment within a school day.

Positioning equipment includes (a) standers designed to provide appropriate support to a student in a standing position, (b) sidelyers that support the student lying on his or her side, (c) supported sitting devices (e.g., corner chairs, bolster chairs) that are specialized chairs to support a student who cannot sit independently, (c) wedges, (d) walkers that encourage walking movements while providing support to the student, as well as numerous other devices.

Regardless of the positioning devices used, it is essential to remember that the goal of using such equipment is to increase meaningful and active participation in ongoing activities within the classroom (Breath, DeMauro, & Snyder, 1997). It is inappropriate to simply place a student in a piece of equipment for a specified period of time. Classroom activities as well as the location of other students influence where and how the student with physical impairments should be positioned. For example, if young students are sitting on the floor for a circle activity, then the student with physical impairments might sit on the floor in a corner chair in order to be at floor level with the others.

As students get older, they tend to spend more time completing class activities at their desks or tables. When students with physical impairments move into middle and high school, they will likely spend more time in their specialized wheelchairs or supported sitting devices at their desks. At this age, it is less likely that they will use adaptive positioning equipment that places them on the floor unless it is for an activity such as physical education. Table 6.1 presents selected classroom activities for various student age groups and adaptive positioning equipment that could be used in those activities. Figure 6.1 provides a sample form for documenting the specific adaptive equipment used by a particular student as well as the activities in which the equipment is used. In this section of the portfolio, photographs of the student positioned correctly in the adaptive equipment can be invaluable to the new educational team.

Table 6.1 Selected Class Activities by Grade Level and Potential Adaptive Equipment

Class Activity	Potential Adaptive Equipment
Preschool and kindergarten activities:	
Arrival and greeting	Specialized wheelchair Walker
Free play	Corner chair on floor Prone over wedge Bolster chair at table Sidelyer
Morning circle	Corner chair
Center activities	Specialized wheelchair Stander Supported sitting device
Story time	Supported sitting device
Departure	Specialized wheelchair
Elementary Activities:	
Arrival and morning recess	Specialized wheelchair Walker
Opening calendar and activities	Supported sitting device (on floor or at desk)
Seatwork activities	Supported sitting device
Free reading	Sidelyer Prone over wedge
Center activities	Supported sitting device Stander
Physical education and recess	Specialized wheelchair Walker
Music	Stander
Middle and high school activities:	
Arrival and changing classes	Specialized wheelchair Walker
Desk activities	Specialized wheelchair Supported sitting device
Physical education	Sidelyer Wedge Stander
Home economics	Stander
Choir	Stander

Figure 6.1 Using Adaptive Equipment in the Classroom

Student: _____   Date: _____

Name of physical therapist:_____   Telephone: _____

Name of occupational therapist:_____   Telephone: _____

• •

Here is a list of the positioning equipment or devices that I use and the activities for which the equipment or devices are used:

EQUIPMENT/DEVICES AND ACTIVITIES	HERE ARE PHOTOGRAPHS OF ME USING EACH PIECE OF EQUIPMENT OR DEVICE AS RECOMMENDED BY THE PT AND/OR OT
1. I use _____ during these activities: _____ _____ _____ _____	
2. I use _____ during these activities: _____ _____ _____ _____	
3. I use _____ during these activities: _____ _____	

Table 6.2 Do's and Don'ts for Appropriate Use of Positioning Equipment

Do	*Don't*
Use equipment to assist the student in being an active participant	Use equipment just to move the student to another position for a specified amount of time
Give the student a meaningful, stimulating activity while using positioning equipment	Leave a student in positioning equipment without a meaningful stimulating activity
Know how to move a student from one piece of equipment to another safely	Move a student from one device to another without first planning and having the equipment conveniently located
Follow therapist's guidelines when using equipment	Use equipment without therapist's recommendation and demonstration
Consider the position of other students when selecting a position for the student with physical impairments	Isolate the student with physical impairments by having the student in a position that limits interactions (e.g., in a sidelyer on the floor when all others are in chairs at desks)

Regardless of the student's age, there are important guidelines to remember when using adaptive positioning equipment in a classroom. Table 6.2 provides examples of Do's and Don't's for appropriate use of positioning equipment.

Using Appropriate "Therapeutic Handling" Techniques

Students with physical impairments are often unable to change positions independently and will require assistance in transferring from one position to another. These students will benefit from therapeutic handling, which involves specialized ways of moving the student that are aimed at facilitating (i.e., increasing) normal muscle tone and movement patterns while inhibiting (i.e., preventing or decreasing) abnormal muscle tone and abnormal or primitive reflexes. Abnormal or primitive reflexes are those reflexes that are present early in life and can interfere with muscle tone and limb movement when they persist past the time when they typically disappear.

For example, for a few months infants with disabilities will display the asymmetric tonic neck (ATNR), or "fencing," reflex. This reflex is elicited by head movement. When the head is turned to the side, the arm and leg on the face side will extend while the arm and leg on the opposite side will

Figure 6.2 Recommendations for Therapeutic Handling

Student: _____ Date: _____
Name of physical therapist:_____ Telephone: _____
Name of occupational therapist:_____ Telephone: _____

• •

Please remember to follow these guidelines when moving me from one
position to another:_____
_____
_____
_____
_____
_____

These photographs or drawings will help you remember how to best use
therapeutic handling with me when engaging in the identified activities:

Activity: _____   Activity: _____

Do	Don't	Do	Don't

Activity: _____   Activity: _____

Do	Don't	Do	Don't

flex or bend. Obviously, if this reflex continues, it will interfere with other independent movements. Unfortunately, some students with physical impairments will continue to display this and other primitive reflexes.

PTs and OTs will recommend appropriate ways of handling a student with physical impairments using the key points of control (i.e., the trunk and area of the body closest to it—head, hips, and shoulders). These key points are the areas of the body that most easily allow the therapists or others to facilitate normal muscle tone while attempting to decrease the effects of reflexes. An example of a form that can be used to identify appropriate therapeutic handling techniques for a specific student is shown in Figure 6.2.

SUMMARY

Using adaptive positioning equipment and therapeutic handling techniques appropriately can be extremely beneficial to students with physical impairments. Such equipment and techniques, which facilitate normal muscle tone and inhibit abnormal patterns of movement, can prevent or decrease permanent changes in muscles or bony structures (e.g., dislocated hips) that can occur in students who have physical impairments. Therefore, this section of the portfolio is very important for these students.

ADDITIONAL RESOURCES

Dormans, J. P., & Pellegrino, L. (1998). *Caring for children with cerebral palsy: A team approach*. Baltimore: Brookes.

Finnie, N. R. (1975). *Handling the young cerebral palsied child at home*. New York: Dutton.

Geralis, E. (Ed.). (1998). *Children with cerebral palsy: A parents' guide* (2nd ed.). Bethesda, MD: Woodbine.

Lutkenhoff, M. (Ed.). (1999). *Children with spina bifida: A parents' guide*. Bethesda, MD: Woodbine.

McCormack, D., B., & Perrin, K. R. (1997*). Spatial, temporal, and physical analysis of motor control: A comprehensive guide to reflexes and reactions*. San Antonio, TX: Therapy Skill Builders.

Communication 7

For the student who is nonverbal or has limited communication skills, it is essential that the portfolio document the student's current receptive and expressive methods of communication. Receptive communication refers to the message that the listener receives and understands from a communication partner. Communication partners can enhance receptive understanding by using various cues paired with spoken words.

Expressive communication is what one person tries to convey to another through the use of body movement, objects, gestures, spoken words, written words, and/or sign language. Both receptive and expressive communication involves multiple forms or methods of communicating. This chapter first discusses portfolio information relevant to methods of enhancing receptive communication. Subsequently, techniques for enhancing expressive communication will be discussed, emphasizing the importance of specifying ongoing opportunities when the student can use his methods of communication. Finally, this chapter will cover strategies for including within the portfolio suggestions for appropriate communication topics as well as documentation of instructional methods designed to expand the student's communication repertoire.

DOCUMENTING THE STUDENT'S RECEPTIVE AND EXPRESSIVE COMMUNICATION

Receptive Communication

For many students with disabilities, it is insufficient to communicate with them only through spoken words due to their difficulties in understanding speech. Spoken words can be accompanied by other cues that provide additional information to these students. Table 7.1 provides a brief description and examples of the types of cues that can enhance receptive communication for the student with limited understanding of speech.

Cues can enhance the meaning of various communicative functions or purposes (e.g., commands, feedback, comments, providing information). For example, a touch cue (e.g., gently tapping the student's shoulder) can be paired with the spoken command, "Sit down." An example of using a

Table 7.1 Descriptions and Examples of Cues That Can Enhance Receptive Communication

Type of Cue	Description of Cue	Example
Touch cues	Cues that are made on a student's body using specific motions or touches	Pressing under the student's arms to cue that the student will be lifted
Object cues	Everyday objects or parts of objects from daily activities used as cues for those activities	Using a bicycle grip to cue bike riding
Olfactory cues	Specific smells that can be associated with activities or people	Smelling shampoo to cue washing hair
Visual cues	Using color, contrast, lighting, spacing, and arrangement of materials to make cues more obvious	Avoiding "busy" backgrounds when presenting objects
Kinesthetic or movement cues	Handling or moving a student in specific ways that are relevant to an upcoming activity	Lifting student's arms above head to cue removing shirt
Auditory or sound cues	Spoken words and environmental sounds	Tapping the table in front of the student to cue that food is there

touch cue paired with spoken words to provide positive feedback could involve rubbing the student's shoulders while saying, "Good job!"

Adding cues will facilitate the student's understanding of familiar activities and events, which will in turn help him or her to anticipate and participate in the activity. Cues can also promote smooth transitions as a result of the student feeling secure about the events to come. In order for cues to be effective in enhancing receptive communication, there are several dos and don'ts to remember (see Table 7.2).

Each person who interacts with the student must use the same cues in order to ensure that the student learns their meaning. These cues are important to document and pass along when the student is changing to a new teacher or school. A diagram such as that in Figure 7.1 can be used as a map to show the location of touch cues as well as the activity or event represented by the touch cue.

In addition, a chart such as that in Figure 7.2 can be used to indicate cues to signal a new activity as well as cues used within that activity. Educational teams should attempt to use cues that enhance various communication purposes (e.g., providing directions, offering feedback, giving information). All of the cues used and the purpose they are conveying should be documented. Whether documenting with a touch cue map or a chart, it is essential that each person who communicates with the student use the same cues *consistently*. Experienced communication partners can

Table 7.2 Do's and Don'ts for Effective Use of Cues to Enhance
Receptive Communication

Do	*Don't*
Select easy and convenient cues	Use complex, cumbersome cues
Select cues that have an obvious relationship to the activity or event represented	Use abstract cues
Select cues that focus the student's attention on the interaction or activity to follow	Use cues that will not be part of the upcoming interaction or activity
Select cues that are pleasant or neutral for the student	Use cues perceived as unpleasant by the student
Use cues immediately before interactions or activities consistently	Be inconsistent
Use firm or deep pressure touch cues	Use light touches as they are typically not well tolerated
Use distinctly different cues to aid discrimination between cues	Use cues that are highly similar to one another
Consider the student's sensory abilities when using visual and auditory cues	Ignore visual and auditory abilities
Use actual objects or parts of objects as cues	Use miniature objects
Consider the student's preferences in choosing olfactory cues	Use smells the student finds unpleasant
Consult with student's PT and/or OT regarding specific recommendations related to positioning and moving the student when using kinesthetic or movement cues	Use movement cues that will negatively affect the student's movement patterns or muscle tone
Keep spoken words simple or use single key words	Use complex spoken words or long sentences

help by modeling the cues for partners who are just beginning to use cues
with the student.

Expressive Communication

As stated previously, strategies for enhancing expressive communication involve techniques for the student with disabilities to convey a message

Figure 7.1   Touch Cue Map

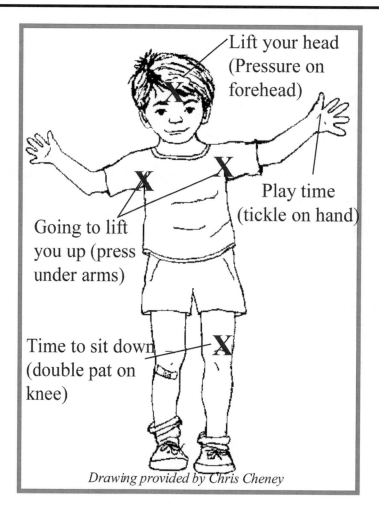

Drawing provided by Chris Cheney

to communication partners. Just as with receptive communication, there are a variety of purposes for expressive communication. For example, the student might have any of the following purposes for communicating:

- Protesting or rejecting
  "I don't like that!"
  "Please stop!"
- Requesting continuation
  "I want more!"
- Making a choice
  "I want a drink." (Not more to eat)
- Greeting others or making social comments
  "Hi!" "Bye!" "Thank you."
- Making offers
  "Would you like some?"
- Providing comments
  "The table is dirty."
- Getting more information
  "What's next?"

Figure 7.2 Documenting Cues for a Specific Activity

Student's name: _____Susie_____   Date: _____11-14-01_____

Activity: _____Brushing teeth after lunch_____

Cue for the activity: _____Have Susie smell the toothpaste_____

Steps for the Activity	Cue
Have Susie open her mouth for the toothbrush	Touch the corner of Susie's mouth with the toothbrush
Wipe Susie's mouth with a cloth	Show Susie the brightly colored washcloth and touch it gently to her cheek
Have Susie take a drink	Show Susie her brightly colored cup and tell her "Drink"

Students with limited communication skills can enhance their expressive messages through a variety of techniques from concrete, pre-symbolic methods to more complex, abstract symbolic methods. Table 7.3 describes three basic categories of behavior that can be used to enhance expressive communication for the student whose verbal communication abilities are limited.

Just as individuals without disabilities typically use multiple methods of communicating (e.g., spoken words paired with gestures, facial expression, and body movements), the student with disabilities will often use more than one method of expressing desired messages. A particular student will express him- or herself in different ways depending upon the situation or the message being communicated. For example, the student might use a gesture (e.g., wave) to say "Hi," but use actual objects when choosing snack foods (e.g., choosing between communication cards that have a cookie and pretzel glued to them) The same student might use photographs of various free time activities to indicate a choice. All of these are examples of Augmentative/Alternative Communication (AAC) options designed to enhance the student's expressive communication.

Some students will use electronic AAC devices that have voice output. AAC voice output devices can range from simple technology (e.g., a loop tape activated by a switch) to more complex (e.g., a sophisticated computer-based system). Voice output devices are often used in combination with

Table 7.3 Categories of Expressive Communication Behaviors

Category	Examples

Pre-symbolic communication:
    Vocalizations
    Body and limb movements
    Simple actions on people
    Simple actions on objects
	Vocalizing to indicate wanting more
	Turning away to indicate "no"
	Pulling a person to a sink to show "drink"
	Banging a cup on the table to show "drink"

Concrete symbolic:
    Symbolic gestures
    Objects
    Photographs
    Line drawings
	Gestures mimicking the shape of a referent
	Actual or parts of objects
	Photos of actual or similar objects or events
	Commercially available sets such as Mayer-Johnson Picture Communication Symbols

Abstract symbolic:
    Speech
    Sign language
    Printed language
	Spoken words
	American Sign Language
	Environmental labeling

some of the symbols highlighted in Table 7.3. For example, objects, photographs, or line drawings could be placed on the voice output device as the symbols the student uses.

Regardless of the level of symbolism used by the student, the expressive communication methods need to be documented. The form in Figure 7.3 can be used as a "Communication Dictionary" to document the student's various forms of expressive communication. The Communication Dictionary is a valuable component of the portfolio, providing new educational teams with readily available information about the student's communication methods.

COMMUNICATION OPPORTUNITIES

In addition to documenting how the student communicates, it is also important to identify the student's communication opportunities. Identifying the activities in which the student can use expressive communication increases the likelihood that communication partners will expect communication efforts from the student. If opportunities are not identified in the portfolio, they may go unrecognized or may be under-utilized by communication partners. Similarly, when the student moves to a new educational setting, valuable time may be unnecessarily used in re-identifying communication opportunities. Incorporated within Figure 7.3 are the activities in which the student uses the various forms of expressive communication.

(Text continues on page 66)

Figure 7.3 Communication Dictionary

Student: _____   Date: _____

____ Yes   ____ No   I use spoken words to communicate.

The following is a list of spoken words that I use now:

_____ _____ _____ _____ _____ _____
_____ _____ _____ _____ _____ _____
_____ _____ _____ _____ _____ _____
_____ _____ _____ _____ _____ _____
_____ _____ _____ _____ _____ _____

____ My words might be hard to understand, please listen to me closely.

____ I can put ____ words together to talk to you.

____ I can use some complete sentences to talk to you.

____ I need ____ seconds before I respond to you.

• •

____ Yes   ____ No   I use sign language to communicate.

The following is a list of signs that I use now:

_____ _____ _____ _____ _____ _____
_____ _____ _____ _____ _____ _____
_____ _____ _____ _____ _____ _____
_____ _____ _____ _____ _____ _____
_____ _____ _____ _____ _____ _____

____ Sometimes my signs might be hard to understand, please watch my signs closely.

____ I can put ____ signs together to communicate to you.

____ I can use some complete sentences to sign to you.

____ I need ____ seconds before I sign back to you.

• •

____ Sometimes I use gestures to communicate.

    ____ I nod my head "yes."

    ____ I shake my head "no."

Figure 7.3 (continued)

_____ I use other gestures:

Gesture:	Communicative Meaning:	Activity:
_____	_____	_____
_____	_____	_____
_____	_____	_____
_____	_____	_____
_____	_____	_____
_____	_____	_____
_____	_____	_____
_____	_____	_____
_____	_____	_____
_____	_____	_____
_____	_____	_____

• •

_____ Sometimes I use objects to tell others what I want. For example, I might hand a cup to someone when I want a drink. These are the objects and communicative meaning that I use as well as the activities in which I use them:

Object:	Communicative Meaning:	Activity:
_____	_____	_____
_____	_____	_____
_____	_____	_____
_____	_____	_____
_____	_____	_____
_____	_____	_____
_____	_____	_____
_____	_____	_____
_____	_____	_____
_____	_____	_____
_____	_____	_____

• •

_____ I use photos / line drawings to communicate. Here are examples of the photos / line drawings that I use:

_____ I have a dictionary of photos / line drawings that I keep with me.

I use photos / line drawings in the following activities:

_____	_____	_____
_____	_____	_____
_____	_____	_____
_____	_____	_____

• •

____ Yes ____ No I use a Voice Output Device to help communicate.

The voice output device(s) I use, the symbols to be placed on the device(s), and the activities in which I use the device(s) and symbols are:

Devices (e.g., BIGmack, Step-by-Step Communicator, Alpha Talker)	Symbols (e.g., objects, photos, line drawings)	Activities (e.g., snack choices, requesting more, story time)
1.		
2.		
3.		
4.		
5.		

• •

Sometimes I use forms of communicating that are not always viewed as communication by others. However, these methods are sometimes the only ways I have to tell others how I feel or what I want.

Figure 7.3 (continued)

Form / Method:	What it means:	Activities I use it in:
____ Cry	_____	_____
____ Aggression	_____	_____
____ Tantrum	_____	_____
____ Self-injury	_____	_____
____ Eye gaze	_____	_____
____ Pull other's hands	_____	_____
____ Touch / Move other's face	_____	_____
____ Grab / Reach	_____	_____
____ Vocalize/ Make noise	_____	_____
____ Remove self / Walk away	_____	_____
____ Facial expressions	_____	_____
____ Change in intonation	_____	_____
____ Other	_____	_____
____ Other	_____	_____
____ Other	_____	_____

COMMUNICATION PARTNERS AND COMMUNICATION TOPICS

Even though the student might have limited verbal communication skills, it is still important that the student communicate with a variety of people. Frequently, peers are overlooked as communication partners and, as a result, only adults communicate with the student using the appropriate AAC methods. The student with disabilities needs to engage in shared experiences with peers who do not have disabilities so they have common subject matter about which to communicate (Durand, Mapstone, & Youngblade, 1999). The form in Figure 7.4 is one way of listing the friends with whom the student spends time and the activities in which they engage. This form also serves to document some basic topics for conversation with the student.

Figure 7.4 Fun Activities and Important People

Student: _____   Date: _____

Here is a list of important family and friends in my life and the activities I enjoy doing with these people:

Name of my friend or family member:	Activities we do together:	Here are photographs of me with my friends or family:

TEACHING COMMUNICATION SKILLS

Obviously, the student with limited communication skills must be taught how to use appropriate AAC options (e.g., providing directions, offering feedback, giving information). Once it is determined which instructional methods work best for the student, it is important to document these methods for the current educational team as well as the new team who will

Figure 7.5   Sample instructional plan for teaching communication skills

INSTRUCTIONAL DOMAIN: *Communication*

OBJECTIVE: *When Jacob needs help to complete an activity, he will point to the "help" card on the ring on his belt loop for 8/10 opportunities for 3/4 consecutive days.*

INSTRUCTIONAL PROMPTS: *Constant Time Delay*
1. *Gently physically assist Jacob to point to "help" card at times help is needed.*
2. *Provide Jacob the first 10 trials at 0-second delay.*
3. *Provide all remaining trials at 4 seconds to provide Jacob with the opportunity to initiate without the physical assistance.*

REINFORCEMENT:

When Jacob points to the "help" card, with or without physical assistance, discreetly provide verbal praise and gently rub his shoulder.

CORRECTIVE FEEDBACK:

If Jacob makes a mistake prior to being given physical assistance, provide the prompt as specified above to facilitate the correct response.

NATURAL TEACHING OPPORTUNITIES:

Whenever Jacob needs help (e.g., coat on/off, assistance to get a drink, various item—desired or needed to complete activities—out of reach.

DATA COLLECTION:
On the data sheet, record a "+" for correct responses with<u>out</u> physical assistance; record "-" for errors or for responses made <u>with</u> physical assistance.

receive the student. There is a wide variety of instructional methods that can be used to teach and expand communication skills, and the form in Figure 7.5 is one way of documenting the most effective ones for a particular student. Although specifically discussing all of the instructional methods relevant to communication skills goes beyond the scope of this book, the resources at the end of the chapter can assist the reader in reviewing these methods as necessary.

SUMMARY

For the student who requires a portion of the portfolio to be devoted to communication, a variety of useful information may be included. This information includes methods for enhancing receptive communication, expressive communication methods used by the student, communication partners and potential communication topics, as well as instructional plans for teaching communication skills.

ADDITIONAL RESOURCES

Bondy, A., & Frost, L. (2002). *A picture's worth: PECS and other visual communication strategies in autism*. Bethesda, MD: Woodbine.

Frost, L. A., & Bondy, A. S. (1994). *The picture exchange communication system: Training manual*. Cherry Hill, NJ: Pyramid Educational Consultants.

Glennen, S. L., & DeCoste, D. C. (1997). *Handbook of augmentative and alternative communication*. San Diego, CA: Singular.

Hodgdon, L. A. (1996). *Visual strategies for improving communication*. Troy, MI: QuirkRoberts.

Korsten, J. E., Dunn, D. K., Foss, T. V., & Francke, M. K. (1993). *Every move counts: Sensory-based communication techniques*. Tucson, AZ: Therapy Skill Builders.

McCarthy, C. F., McLean, L. K., Miller, J. F., Paul-Brown, D., Romski, M. A., Rourk, J. D., & Yoder, D. E. (1998). *Communication supports checklist for programs serving individuals with severe disabilities*. Baltimore: Brookes.

McClannahan, L. E., & Krantz, P. J. (1999). *Activity schedules for children with autism: Teaching independent behavior*. Bethesda, MD: Woodbine.

Reichle, J., Beukelmand, D. R., & Light, J. C. (2002). *Exemplary practices for beginning communicators: Implications for AAC*. Baltimore: Brookes.

Rowland, C., & Schweigert, P. (2000). *Tangible symbol systems: Making the right to communicate a reality for individuals with severe disabilities* (2nd ed.). Portland: Oregon Health Sciences University.

8

Behavior Support and Reinforcement Strategies

E ven if the student does not display problem behaviors, this section of the portfolio should include information about effective reinforcement strategies so that new teams do not have to re-explore to determine what motivates the student. Thus, this chapter will first discuss documenting effective reinforcement strategies.

That said, this section of a portfolio is especially relevant for the student who has problem behavior(s) *in addition* to having a disability or as part of the disability. In order to be effective in supporting the student with behavior problems, it is essential that all team members respond to these problems in the same way. When the student moves to a new educational situation, the receiving team will benefit immeasurably from knowing what was successful in the past in terms of dealing with problem behavior.

To develop effective behavior support plans, the educational team must first complete a functional behavior assessment. This chapter will focus on documenting the results of a functional behavior assessment and using those results to develop a positive behavioral support plan. Elements of successful positive behavioral support plans will be reviewed.

EFFECTIVE REINFORCEMENT STRATEGIES

This section of the portfolio is useful for listing the type of reinforcer(s) the student prefers, as well as information regarding how the reinforcers should be delivered to the student. For example, some students like public, enthusiastic praise, while other students would be mortified by such praise and prefer that it be communicated discreetly. Providing information about effective reinforcement strategies will help new team members to interact

Figure 8.1 Reinforcement Strategies

The type of reinforcement I prefer is:

____ Social   ____ Activities   ____Tangible objects ____ Food/Drinks
____ Verbal ____ Other:_____

Here is a description of reinforcing *social interactions* **that works with me:**

Here is a description of reinforcing *activities* **that work with me:**

Here is a description of reinforcing *tangible objects* **that work with me:**

Here is a description of reinforcing *food/drinks* **that work with me:**

Verbal praise **is most effective when delivered in this manner:**
_____ Very enthusiastic, public praise

_____ Fairly enthusiastic, public praise

_____ Quiet, privately delivered praise

_____ Neutrally (no voice fluctuatation)

Additional comments about my reinforcers:

successfully with the student without the necessity of re-identifying effective reinforcers. Figure 8.1 offers a sample form for documenting effective reinforcers.

FUNCTIONAL BEHAVIOR ASSESSMENT

Underlying Assumptions

Prior to discussing how to include the results of a functional behavior assessment in a portfolio, it is important to understand the fundamental assumptions that underlie this approach to responding to problem behaviors (Demchak & Bossert, 1996). First, all behavior has a purpose or function; the student engages in problem behavior for a specific reason. Common functions of problem behavior include (a) to gain attention of peers or adults, (b) to escape an activity or task, (c) to avoid an activity or task, (d) to gain access to a tangible object or activity, and (e) to obtain sensory stimulation. The second assumption is that problem behavior serves a communicative purpose. That is, the student, based on the functions listed, is communicating a message (e.g., *"I want you to pay attention to me." "I don't like this activity." "I'm bored."*). In many instances, it is easier for the student, even

Table 8.1   Important Assumptions Underlying Functional Assessment of Behavior

1.   Problem behavior serves a purpose.

2.   Problem behavior communicates a message.

3.   Problem behavior does *not* occur in isolation but is connected to events in the environment.

4.   The same problem behavior can serve multiple purposes for the student.

the student who has verbal skills, to communicate this message via problem behavior than through more conventional communication strategies. The third important assumption is that behavior does not occur in a vacuum; that is, it is connected to events occurring in the student's environment. For example, what happens before and after the behavior influences the occurrence of the behavior. Finally, it is essential to remember that one behavior can serve more than one purpose for the student. For example, in one class the student may hit a peer as a way of attempting to escape a nonpreferred activity. At recess, the same student might hit a peer to gain the peer's attention in order to play. Table 8.1 summarizes these important underlying assumptions.

Completing a Functional Behavior Assessment

To conduct a comprehensive functional behavior assessment, there are several steps that the educational team must follow. (This section will outline the basic steps involved in the process rather than provide a detailed explanation. See Demchak & Bossert [1996] or other resources listed for a more in-depth discussion.)

Identify Problem Behaviors. This step involves listing any problem behaviors as well as the situations in which they occur and do *not* occur. This information is typically gathered by interviewing significant others (e.g., family members, teachers, paraeducators) who know the student well.

Prioritize Problem Behaviors. It is not unusual for the student to have more than one problem behavior. If this is the case, the educational team must prioritize the behaviors to determine which of them warrant immediate assessment and behavior support plan development and which are minor and require only monitoring. Behaviors that call for immediate action by the team include those that threaten the physical well-being of the student or others, interfere with the learning process for the student or others, damage or destroy materials in the setting, or interfere with interactions with and acceptance by peers. In other instances, the prioritization process might lead the educational team to encourage team members to be more tolerant and to realize that behavior support plans are not needed for all behaviors. For example, a classroom teacher may simply need to be more tolerant of the student who sits at the desk with one leg tucked under her bottom on the chair. This is an example of a very minor situation that does not merit an assessment and development of a support plan.

Define Problem Behaviors. Now that the educational team has determined which behaviors, if any, warrant a functional behavior assessment, those behaviors must be defined in observable and measurable terms. In other words, the team must come up with an "operational definition." An operational definition ensures that everyone is focusing on the same behavior and that it is clearly defined and not open to interpretation. For example, stating that the student displays "disruptive behavior" can mean different things to each person who observes. However, stating specifically that the student "throws work materials" is much more precise and increases the likelihood that team members will be observing the same behavior as part of the functional behavior assessment process.

Formulate Hypotheses. The fourth step is much more complex than the previous steps of the functional behavior assessment process. This step focuses on gathering specific information about the operationally defined problem behaviors in order to aid the team in forming a hypothesis about the function or purpose of the behavior. Methods of gathering specific information that are particularly useful and manageable for educational team members include (a) completing structured interviews and discussing the situation as a team, (b) completing scatter plots, and (c) conducting ABC (Antecedent-Behavior-Consequences) analyses. The results of these assessment methods will help the team to focus on those environmental variables that might be influencing the behavior. A hypothesis could relate to any of the previously mentioned common functions of problem behavior (e.g., attention, escape, avoidance, tangibles, sensory feedback).

Gathering information through structured interviews (see Demchak and Bossert, 1996; O'Neill et al., 1997) helps the team to focus on (a) specific situations in which the behavior is most likely to occur, (b) situations in which the behavior does not occur, (c) potential antecedent events (i.e., those that may immediately precede the behavior), (d) potential setting events (i.e., those events such as lack of sleep that are more distant from occurrences of the behavior), (e) consequences that follow the behavior, as well as (f) potential effective reinforcers. Unfortunately, it is rarely sufficient to rely only on the results of structured interviews to form hypotheses about problem behaviors. It is also necessary to conduct direct observations of the behaviors.

Direct observations can be done using scatter plots and ABC analyses. Scatter plots can reveal patterns in activities and times of day in which the behavior is more likely (or less likely) to occur. Scatter plots are made on a grid form with days of the week on the horizontal axis and times of day on the vertical axis (see Demchak & Bossert, 1996). Observers make slash marks in each time period to indicate the number of times a particular behavior occurred. The team can then review these data collected over several days for patterns in when the behavior does or does not occur.

Identifying these patterns can help the team predict occurrences of problem behaviors and then prevent behaviors from occurring by modifying problem situations.

ABC analyses involve note taking in which the observer writes down exactly what happened immediately prior and immediately following the behavior. These notes are typically transferred to a form with columns (i.e., one column each for the antecedents, behavior, and consequences). After data are collected for several consecutive days, the team reviews them for patterns in the immediate antecedents and consequences.

The team reviews the results of the structured interviews, scatter plots, and ABC analyses to write hypothesis, or summary, statements about the function, or purpose, of the problem behavior. A comprehensive hypothesis statement includes three components: (a) when *blank* happens (i.e., the antecedent and setting events), (b) the student does *blank* (i.e., the problem behavior), (c) in order to *blank* (i.e., the purpose of the behavior) (Bambara & Knoster, 1998). These statements then guide the development of a positive behavior support plan by specifically linking the functional behavior assessment results to the behavior support plan. A summary of a functional behavior assessment is shown in Figure 8.2. This type of summary should be included in the student's portfolio to aid others who work with the student.

Developing a Positive Behavior Support Plan

Based on the functional assessment results and the hypothesis statements, the educational team develops a comprehensive behavior support plan that contains (a) the operational definition, (b) the hypothesis or summary statements, (c) setting event strategies, (d) antecedent strategies, (e) replacement behaviors the student will be taught, (f) consequence strategies, (g) crisis management strategies, (h) generalization and maintenance strategies, and (i) procedures for ongoing monitoring and evaluation (Demchak & Elquist, 2001). All team members should then implement this behavior support plan consistently. Having the plan in writing makes it more likely that it will be implemented as intended, which will in turn make it more likely that the student's problem behaviors will decrease, while appropriate alternative behaviors will increase.

Operational Definitions and Hypothesis Statements. The operational definition and hypothesis statements are repeated on the behavior support plan in case it is the only document readily available to a team member. Repeating this vital information ensures that the team members have access to it when implementing the behavior support plan.

Setting Event Strategies. Setting events are those events that are more distant than antecedents from an occurrence of problem behavior, but still influence the behavior. A few common examples of setting events are fatigue due to going to bed late, hunger due to skipping a meal, and illness. Everyone has had the experience of being irritable as a result of not feeling

Figure 8.2 Sample Summary of a Functional Behavior Assessment

Problem behaviors displayed:

Hitting peers and answering teacher questions without being called on.

Prioritization:

Hitting peers was an immediate priority because the behavior could potentially harm others and interfered with peer acceptance. Answering without being called on was not a priority because the behavior actually occurred infrequently.

Operational definition:

Hitting peers with an open or closed hand.

Structured interview results:

Hitting occurred (a) in situations in which the teacher was attending to other students, (b) when other students were in Jason's space (i.e., too close to him), (c) during activities that are disliked by Jason. It was also thought that Jason was more likely to hit peers if he had skipped breakfast that morning (i.e., he seemed more irritable). He liked free time.

Scatter plot results:

Hitting consistently occurred each morning during math groups and independent math seatwork. It also occurred consistently during silent sustained reading after lunch.

ABC analysis results:

During math, consistent antecedent events included requests to answer verbally or in writing specific math facts. A consistent consequence during math was that the teacher would give Jason extra assistance during group work and remove his work during independent seatwork so that he did not have to complete it. During sustained silent reading, Jason would be told to put his book away and to wait quietly.

Hypothesis statements:

1. *When Jason has skipped breakfast, it is more likely that he will hit peers who are within 2 feet of him in order to get them to move farther away.*
2. *When Jason is asked to complete math facts during group work, he hits peers to gain teacher assistance.*
3. *When Jason is asked to complete math facts during independent seatwork, he hits peers to escape the task.*
4. *When Jason is asked to read during sustained silent reading, he hits peers to escape the task.*

well (and perhaps displaying what others would call problem behavior). Strategies in this component of the behavior support plan are aimed at identifying setting events that could precede problem behaviors and techniques for responding to them.

Antecedent Strategies. Antecedent events are those that are more immediate (in comparison to setting events) to an occurrence of problem behavior. Strategies in this area can include (a) removing a problem activity, (b) modifying an activity or task likely to influence problem behavior, (c) intermingling difficult and nonpreferred activities with easy and preferred activities, (d) adding activities to the schedule that are associated with desired behaviors, and (e) minimizing the impact of nonpreferred activities as much as possible (e.g., allow breaks) (Bambara & Knoster, 1998).

Teaching Replacement Behaviors. Teaching an appropriate replacement behavior that matches the purpose of the problem behavior is an essential component of a behavior support plan. For example, if Jason hits peers during group math to get assistance from the teacher, then he needs to learn an alternative means of asking for attention. This section of the portfolio specifies the target replacement behavior(s) as well as important guidelines to remember.

In order to be effective, it is essential that the replacement behavior (a) match the purpose of the problem behavior; (b) be at least as easy, if not easier, for the student to perform as the problem behavior was; and (c) be at least as effective in achieving its purpose as the problem behavior was (i.e., it elicits as quick and consistent a response as the problem behavior did). Considering these variables in selecting a replacement behavior will likely improve the team's success in increasing desired behavior while decreasing the occurrence of the problem behavior.

Consequence Strategies. Consequences refer to what happens after an occurrence of the problem behavior as well as what happens after an occurrence of the desired replacement behavior. When responding to occurrences of the problem behavior, it is essential that everyone understand the function of the behavior because some common consequences, or responses, could be inappropriate. For example, if the student engages in problem behavior for the purpose of escaping an activity, then using timeout as a consequence would be counterproductive. Likewise, if the student engages in problem behavior to gain teacher attention, then providing attention, even in the form of reprimands, would be inappropriate. Thus, it is essential for the team to consider the function of the problem behavior when specifying consequences for an occurrence of the behavior.

In addition to stating how to respond to problem behavior, the support plan should also detail how to respond to the replacement behavior when it occurs. Everyone should respond immediately and consistently, but the support plan can provide more specific details as to the most effective response to use with a particular student

Crisis Management Strategies. Behaviors that threaten the safety and well-being of the student or others will require crisis management strategies that protect the student and others. Such strategies might include removing other students from the setting, moving furniture, or moving objects out of reach. Please note that if physical restraint is to be used as part of

Figure 8.3   Sample Completed Behavior Support Plan

Operational definition of problem behaviors:

Hitting peers with an open or closed hand.

Hypothesis statements:

1.   *When Jason has skipped breakfast, it is more likely that he will hit peers who are within 2 feet of him in order to get them to move farther away.*
2.   *When Jason is asked to complete math facts during group work, he hits peers to gain teacher assistance.*
3.   *When Jason is asked to complete math facts during independent seatwork, he hits peers to escape the task.*
4.   *When Jason is asked to read during sustained silent reading, he hits peers to escape the task.*

Setting event strategies:

Have nutritional snacks available for those mornings that Jason does not have breakfast.

Antecedent strategies:

Avoid giving math facts as independent work; provide a calculator for Jason to use.
Provide Jason with an alternative sustained silent reading activity (e.g., listening to books on tape, listening to a peer partner read).

Replacement behavior(s):

Instruct Jason to ask peers to "please move" if they are too close to him.
Instruct Jason to ask for teacher assistance during group math.

Consequence strategies:

Respond to all requests for teacher assistance immediately and consistently.
Prompt peers to respond to Jason's requests immediately and consistently.

Provide corrective feedback (No, don't hit!).
Take away free time when he hits.
Do not use timeout, given the escape function of Jason's behaviors.

Crisis management strategies:

Given the lack of severity of Jason's hitting behaviors, crisis management is not needed. However, if hitting were to escalate, then have peers leave the area.

Generalization and maintenance strategies:

Ensure implementation of plan by general and special education teachers in all settings.

Monitoring and evaluation:

Collect data three times each week on both problem behaviors and replacement behaviors. Evaluate data weekly to determine if changes are needed in the plan.

Table 8.2   Important Do's and Don'ts

Do	*Don't*
Complete a comprehensive functional assessment prior to developing a support plan	Develop a support plan without assessment results on which to base supports
Match replacement behaviors to the purpose of the problem behavior	Arbitrarily select replacement behaviors
Select replacement behaviors that are at least as easy to do as the problem behavior is	Select more difficult replacement behaviors
Respond immediately and consistently to replacement behaviors	Ignore replacement behaviors
Regularly collect data on replacement behaviors and problem behaviors	Implement behavior support plans without regularly monitoring effectiveness
Evaluate data routinely to determine if changes to the plan are needed	Collect data without regular review

crisis management, the person implementing it *must* receive training from certified trainers *prior* to the use of restraint. The use of physical restraint is prohibited by state law or by school district policy in some locations. In other instances, it might only be allowed if included as part of a comprehensive support plan that is addressed within the student's IEP and parent/guardian permission has been granted.

Generalization and Maintenance Strategies. To increase the likelihood that there will comprehensive improvements in the student's behavior, it is important to ensure that generalization and maintenance are addressed. Generalization refers to making certain that the behavior support plan is implemented across settings (e.g., various locations within the school, home, and community) and across people (e.g., all team members, family members, peers). Maintenance refers to implementing strategies for sustaining improvements over time.

Monitoring and Evaluation. A positive behavior support plan must include data that are collected on the problem behavior as well as on the replacement behavior. Collecting data is the only way of guaranteeing that the behavior support plan is having the desired effect (i.e., the problem behavior is decreasing and the replacement behavior is increasing). However, it is insufficient simply to collect data; they must also be evaluated regularly so that appropriate changes can be made to the support plan.

A completed behavior support plan is shown in Figure 8.3. Including a support plan in the portfolio increases the likelihood that any problem behaviors are being responded to appropriately. However, it is essential that team members remember to update functional behavior assessments and the behavior support plan itself when the student moves to a new setting.

SUMMARY

The portfolio section dealing with effective reinforcers can be invaluable to teams receiving all students with disabilities. However, for the student who has behavior problems, information about effective reinforcers, as well as the summary of the functional behavior assessment and the behavior support plan, are essential. Table 8.2 summarizes important Dos and Don'ts to remember when developing this section of the portfolio.

ADDITIONAL RESOURCES

Horner, R. H., Albin, R. W., Sprague, J. R., & Todd, A. W. (2000). Positive behavior support. In M. E. Snell & F. Brown (Eds.), *Instruction of students with severe disabilities* (5th ed., pp. 207-244). Upper Saddle River, NJ: Merrill.

Lucyshyn, J. M., Dunlap, G., & Albin, R. W. (2002). *Families and positive behavior support: Addressing problem behaviors in family contexts.* Baltimore: Brookes.

Repp, A. C., & Horner, R. H. (Eds.). (1999). *Functional analysis of problem behavior: From effective assessment to effective support.* Belmont, CA: Wadsworth.

Scotti, J. R., & Meyer, L. H. (Eds.). (1999). *Behavioral intervention: Principles, models, and practices.* Baltimore: Brookes.

9

Teaming, Problem Solving, and Keeping Notes

Teamwork plays an important role in designing a school program for the student with a disability. Many of the students who can benefit from a transition portfolio have various people, including teachers, therapists, psychologists, and administrators, involved in their school life. But working with the student on an individual basis and being a member of the student's collaborative team is different from simply being present in the student's school life. This chapter will describe the elements of an effective collaborative team and how a portfolio is a useful tool for documenting a team's decisions and program planning.

ELEMENTS OF AN EFFECTIVE COLLABORATIVE TEAM

The student's team should be designed to meet the needs of the individual. In the past, teams simply consisted of people who understood the student's disability. They may have been trained to work in a multidisciplinary model in which team members develop separate plans for intervention within their own discipline. The move to include students with disabilities in various settings has changed the face of school teams. It has created a more collaborative team atmosphere in schools that has benefited not only students, but also team members (Downing, 2002; Thousand & Villa, 1992). The makeup of teams has changed to be more personal and includes people who are interested in various facets of the student, not just the student's disability. General education teachers, paraprofessionals, peers, and the students themselves play more of a role in this kind of teaming approach.

Developing an effective team is not an easy task. It requires a partnership among team members and a vision for the future of the student. Team members must be able to work interdependently and in a transdisciplinary manner. They must be supportive of one another and be practicing group problem-solvers. To operate in an effective manner the team must also create a structure that promotes collaboration. This includes scheduling regular opportunities for team members to meet, developing guidelines for keeping the team organized and making decisions, using problem-solving strategies, and regularly evaluating team effectiveness.

Scheduling Meeting Times

Time is an issue for everyone. It is therefore important for the student's team to be creative and develop alternate modes of sharing information. For example, sometimes a "core" team is developed that includes people who see the student on a daily basis, such as the special education teacher, the general education teacher, and the paraprofessional. The core team meets every week to problem solve and discuss the student's program.

A second tier of the team structure might include school personnel who see the student on a regular, but not daily, basis. This tier may consist of a speech language pathologist, an occupational therapist, a vision specialist, as well as representatives of other disciplines. The second-tier group may join with the core team and meet formally on a quarterly basis, or as needed. These meetings would also include the student's family and his or her classroom peers.

For example, Jane's core team consists of Mrs. Conrad, the special education teacher; Mr. Jackson, her third-grade teacher; and Beth, the support person who is with her in the classroom each day. As the school year began, Mrs. Conrad conducted an observation of the third-grade classroom and interviewed Mr. Jackson. She also got a copy of the weekly schedule. Mrs. Conrad made sure she kept this information so she could include it in Jane's transition portfolio.

The team decided to meet for 15 minutes every Monday morning to discuss Jane's program and how she was going to participate in the weekly activities of the class. Mrs. Bailey, the speech and language pathologist, joins the team every other week to talk about Jane's augmentative communication system and how she is using it in the classroom and school in general. Jane's core team has become very efficient during the meeting time. They make sure to talk about specific areas of success and concern and always leave the meeting with an action plan (Figure 9.1).

The second tier of Jane's team meets three times a year to discuss her program. One of these meetings focuses specifically on her IEP. This meeting brings Jane's whole team, including her parents, together to discuss her program and update her MAPS. Although the yearly schedule is created in September, the team has agreed that they can get together for an unscheduled meeting anytime a member feels the team needs to discuss an issue.

Figure 9.1 Team Action Plan

What Needs to Be Done?	Who Will Do It?	Time Frame
1) Call Mr. Hall, district vision consultant to arrange vision update for Jane.	Mrs. Conrad (Special Ed teacher)	Completed by Sept 12
2) Talk to MedCenter about the foot pedals on Jane's wheelchair.	Mr. Hulett (OT)	Completed by Oct 1- call Mrs. Conrad Arranged by Oct 1
3) Organize a "Circle of Friends" session with 3rd-grade class.	Miss Hansen (Jane's assistant)	Completed by September 23
4) Call United Cerebral Palsy and order switches.	Mrs. Colter (Speech-language pathologist)	

GETTING ORGANIZED AND MAKING DECISIONS

One of the key elements in creating an efficient collaborative team is to be organized and able to make decisions as a group. Although there are certain general guidelines for making a meeting run smoothly, the rules of conduct need to be established by the team members themselves. Here are several questions that might be asked before a meeting takes place.

1. Who will facilitate the meeting?
2. Who will develop the agenda?
3. Who will take, type, and mail the notes taken at the meeting?
4. Who will be the "jargon buster" and remind people to use generic language?
5. How much time will be set aside for the meeting?
6. Who will be the timekeeper?
7. How will the team resolve issues?

Taking the time to design structures for conducting a meeting will assist with the process and create positive outcomes for team members and for students (Romer & Byrne, 1995). Making decisions and resolving conflicts is part of the developmental process of becoming an effective team (Bailey, 1984). All teams have their growing pains and need to be cognizant of the interpersonal and group identity factors that operate within small groups.

COLLABORATIVE PROBLEM SOLVING

Designing a meaningful program for the student with a disability can be challenging. A number of issues can arise and create conflict or confusion for a team. For example, team members may not understand or agree on how to include the student in different settings or activities. Or they may be "stuck" on how to deal with a disruptive behavior. It is therefore important that team members have the skills to solve problems in a positive and effective manner.

There are a variety of problem-solving strategies that can be used to assist a team in meeting student and professional challenges. The Osborn-Parnes Creative Problem-Solving (CPS) process (Parnes 1981, 1992) is one method used by teachers to assist them in designing programs for students with disabilities. The CPS process describes the characteristics of people who are good problem solvers. These characteristics include the following:

- Problem solvers believe everyone is creative and has the capacity to solve problems.
- Problem solvers are optimistic.
- Problem solvers alternate between divergent and convergent thinking.
- Problem solvers actively defer and engage their judgment.
- Problem solvers encourage "free-wheeling" and fun.
- Problem solvers take action.

Teams who use this process go through different stages that include objective finding, fact finding, problem finding, idea finding, solution finding, and acceptance finding. During the objective-finding stage of the process, a team will consider various challenges they face with a student or at the school, then choose one they think they can begin to solve. The fact-finding stage requires team members to list different facts about the problem. This should be a quick-paced exercise that focuses on the "who, what, where, when, why, and how" questions about the challenge. The problem-finding stage requires team members to clarify the problem by redefining the challenge in positive and different words (e.g., "In what ways might we help Jane be more of a participant?"). This step assists the team in understanding what they want to accomplish by solving the problem. During the idea-finding stage, the team members generate as many ideas as possible to solve the challenge. The solution-finding stage involves defining criteria for selecting solutions to the problem that have been generated by the team (e.g., feasibility, time factors, efficient for the teacher to use). The final stage of the process is acceptance-finding. The objective of this stage is to design an action plan that includes the ideas generated by the team members. The Osborn-Parnes strategy is powerful and encourages people who use it to incorporate it into their daily lives.

There are several variations of CPS (Giangreco, Cloninger, Dennis, & Edelman, 1994) that can be established quickly and adapted to any small group who is problem solving about a particular issue. The first variation is aimed at a team of students who are problem solving about another student (see Box 9.1).

**BOX 9.1   STEPS IN THE "ONE-MINUTE
IDEA-FINDING" OR "ASK KIDS" STRATEGY**

Step 1. The team facilitator or teacher presents an issue or directions for an activity. This provides the group/class with some information about the challenge (i.e., fact finding).

Step 2. The team facilitator or teacher presents the challenge to the team or class. For example, the team facilitator may say, "We need to try and figure out how Jane can participate in the Pledge of Allegiance each morning," or a teacher may say, "Let's figure out how everyone can be included in the history project." This step combines objective finding and problem finding.

Step 3. The team or class has one minute to generate ideas in an atmosphere of deferred judgment. Each idea is valued and considered by the group. This is the idea-finding stage of the CPS process. Ideas are recorded on the chalkboard or on chart paper.

Step 4. The team or class members select the ideas they wish to use. This is the solution-finding stage.

Step 5. The students participate in the activity and use the idea. This last step is the acceptance-finding stage of CPS.

When using any problem-solving strategy, it is important to remember the purpose of the strategy, which is to create a quality educational experience for the student. There are certain questions that team members may need to ask themselves regarding how the student is included in a particular activity. For example, can the student "partially participate" (Baumgart et al., 1982; Ferguson & Baumgart, 1991) in an activity? Does the activity involve a skill the student will use in the future? How important is it to the student or his family that he be involved in the activity?

Finally, it is always a good idea for team members to evaluate the process they have used to make decisions and how well the strategies they have developed have worked for the student. Using a quick method such as a "Kaizen" (Figure 9.2) can help team members share their perceptions of the success of the current meeting as well as discuss changes needed for future meetings. In addition, it is important that team members have access to any classroom data so they can review the effectiveness of the student's educational program.

WRITING IT ALL DOWN

This section of the portfolio creates a place for team members to include their meeting notes (Figure 9.3) as well as their rationale for making decisions (Figure 9.4). Keeping a record of meeting notes allows new school personnel to retrace the previous team's steps. Meeting notes can provide relevant information about important topics, continuing challenges, actions taken, and solutions that worked for the student and the team.

The team should also keep a written record of their problem-solving processes and the rationale behind their decisions. For example, Jane is currently using her augmentative communication device to participate in the class's daily recitation of the Pledge of Allegiance. She pushes a button

Figure 9.2 Kaizen

+	−
"The whole team was present at the meeting."	"Not everyone contributed to the conversation."
"The team has a very positive attitude about Jane's program."	"We need to try and not divert from the agenda."
"The tasks have been evenly assigned. This is really a team effort."	
"Jane's family is very involved in her program."	

Figure 9.3 Team Meeting Notes

Student: Jane Hopkins   Date: September 15, 2001

Team members: **Position:**

Ellen Hopkins	Jane's mother
Lucy Conrad	Resource room teacher
Ann Jackson	Third-grade teacher
Susan Colter	Speech-language pathologist
Terry Hansen	Jane's assistant
Brian Hulett	Occupational therapist

Roles:

Facilitator:	Lucy Conrad
Recorder:	Brian Hulett
Timekeeper:	Terry Hansen
Jargonbuster:	Susan Colter

Agenda for this meeting:	Time Limit:
Update on Jane's current medical issues	10 minutes
Review Jane's communication system	15 minutes
Jane's social network	15 minutes
New issues in 3rd grade	10 minutes
Action plan/Next meeting time	10 minutes

Figure 9.3 (continued)

Team Meeting Notes – September 15, 2001

The meeting began at 2:45 p.m. The team has allowed an hour for the meeting. Mrs. Conrad and Mrs. Hopkins gave the team an update on Jane's current state of health. Jane is currently on Tegretol for seizures but has not had a seizure for the past year. Her general health is good. Jane has not had a vision evaluation for two years and her mother would like the district vision consultant to conduct a functional vision exam within the next month.

Jane's current communication system consists of using a calendar system with tangible objects to represent activities of the school day and an augmentative device. This system seems to be working well, but Mrs. Colter would like to add another kind of switch so that Jane can make more choices and access her tape player. The school does not have many switches, so Mrs. Colter is going to try and find a place that will lend the school some switches.

The team members are concerned that Jane needs to be more involved in the life of the third grade. Since this is a new school with a new group of children, the team would like to figure out a way to connect Jane with her peers. Mrs. Hopkins suggested conducting a "Circle of Friends" session with the class. She said this had been done at Jane's previous school and had worked well. The team agreed that this was a good idea and should be done as quickly as possible.

The meeting ended at 3: 40. The next meeting is scheduled for January 7, 2002.

Figure 9.4 Team Decision-Making Log

September 2001

Jane has been participating in the Pledge of Allegiance by pushing a button on her communication device that says the Pledge using a child's computerized voice. Jane's team does not currently think this is a priority skill and has decided that she should use her device to "begin" the Pledge and learn a skill that she can use across multiple environments.

---

and a computerized child's voice says the Pledge along with the class. Jane's teacher wonders if there is a better way for Jane to participate in this activity. The team, including Jane's family, does not feel the Pledge of Allegiance is a priority skill in Jane's life but would still like to figure out some way for her to participate. The teacher brings this issue to the team meeting, and as a result, the team decides that it would be more beneficial for Jane to use her communication device to say "Ready? Begin," rather than to say the entire Pledge. Team members also came up with other environments and events that take place throughout the week where Jane can use her device to begin an activity.

SUMMARY

A portfolio is a useful tool for documenting the program of the student with a disability. Team members work hard to create effective programs for students and often make decisions based on parent preference or other team member input. Teams who keep notes about their decisions can help future teams from "reinventing the wheel" and wasting valuable instructional time.

ADDITIONAL RESOURCES

Creating collaborative IEPs: A handbook. (1998). Richmond: VA Institute for Developmental Disabilities, Virginia Commonwealth University.

Friend, M., & Cook, L. (2000). *Interactions: Collaboration skills for school professionals* (3rd ed.). White Plains, NY: Longman.

Rainforth, B., & York-Barr, J. (1997). *Collaborative teams for students with severe disabilities.* Baltimore: Brookes.

Snell, M. E., & Janney, R. (2000). *Teacher's guides to inclusive practices: Collaborative teaming.* Baltimore: Brookes.

Thousand, J. S., Villa, R. A., & Nevin, A. I. (1994). *Creativity and collaborative learning: A practical guide to empowering students and teachers.* Baltimore: Brookes.

Final Thoughts

A transition portfolio can be a valuable tool for teachers and families of students with disabilities. Although the student's IEP is meant to act as a guide for programming, it is not able to document the subtle pieces of information that can assist teachers and other team members in making the student's daily instruction as effective as possible.

A transition portfolio should provide a resource for the student's new teachers, paraeducators, and other team members. It should give the team the kind of information that is critical to the student's daily activities (e.g., impact of medication, communication strategies), as well as provide a specific place to keep track of this information on an ongoing basis. Students with disabilities encounter many professionals as they go through the school system, and these professionals often pass along things they have learned about a student. But their notes and data may be lost when the teacher or other support personnel leaves the team. Each of the previous team's small discoveries, that can easily be lost in a transition, can have a definitive impact on the student's daily interactions with peers and team members. For example, by reading the communication section of a portfolio, a team can learn how the student communicates through subtle body movements and gestures. Instead of ignoring the student or misreading the communicative intent, team members will have the information they need to respond to the student's communication efforts in a positive manner.

At the beginning of this book, we introduced Susie as she was about to leave preschool and enter kindergarten. Her preschool teacher, Ms. Black, developed a transition portfolio that she shared with Susie's new teacher *prior* to Susie starting kindergarten. As a result, Mr. Anderson, the kindergarten teacher, knew important information about Susie on the very first day of school. He did not lose valuable time trying to figure out how to interact with Susie and how to teach her. He knew how to recognize and respond to Susie's communication as well as how to convey information to her. He also knew how to best interact with Susie in order to make maximum use of her limited vision and hearing. The adaptations and instructional strategies developed and used to teach Susie in preschool also proved to be relevant in kindergarten. Mr. Anderson has expressed his appreciation for the transition portfolio to Ms. Black and to Susie's parents numerous times. Because he and the other team members have seen how useful and valuable a transition portfolio can be, they are updating Susie's on a regular basis so that it will be ready to share with her first-grade teacher.

Students with disabilities begin their school careers with their own unique abilities, strengths, and needs. Each student, no matter what his or her disability, deserves to receive a quality education. Developing a transition portfolio is one way to assure that a student's team has the kind of information it needs to create a successful program.

Appendix A

Susie's Case Study

OVERVIEW

Susie Johnson will soon be 6 years old and in the fall will go to kindergarten. She has had the same preschool teacher for the last 3 years. As a result, Ms. Black knows Susie quite well. Susie really enjoyed preschool with its frequently changing activities, especially music, art activities, and snack time. She especially liked the "enthusiastic" play of some of her friends. Susie is like her preschool classmates in many ways. However, she is also different in that she has severe, multiple disabilities that make her transition to kindergarten more complex than it will be for the majority of her classmates. Susie's disabilities include cognitive and motor impairments, limited communication skills, a hearing loss, and cortical visual impairment.

In late April of Susie's last year in preschool, her parents and teacher attended a two-day conference for parents of children with multiple disabilities. At this conference, they heard about compiling transition portfolios for students who were moving on to new teachers for any number of reasons. Mr. and Mrs. Johnson and Ms. Black came away very excited about compiling a transition portfolio for Susie. However, they only had about one month remaining in the school year and needed to work quickly. They set priorities and decided that the sections of the transition portfolio that should be completed prior to the end of the school year were the following:

1. Medical information

2. Educational programming (an IEP summary)

3. Adaptations needed

4. Communication strategies

5. Reinforcement strategies

The sample in this case study includes the results of this priority planning. Mr. and Mrs. Johnson are committed to the process and plan to add to the transition portfolio during Susie's kindergarten year so that the first-grade teacher receives a more complete portfolio. For example, they want to include an instructional matrix, classroom participation plans with suggestions for adaptations, considerations for Susie's physical impairments, as well as more information regarding communication (specifically, conversation topics and important people in Susie's life). Mr. and Mrs. Johnson would also like to complete the MAPS process with Susie's new educational team near the beginning of the school year. However, given the limited time they had remaining in the school year when they learned about transition portfolios, they were thrilled with what they were able to accomplish and have ready for the kindergarten teacher.

Portfolio Cover Sheet

Initial portfolio date: *May 30, 2001*

My name is: *Susie Johnson*

My birthday is: *June 15*   I am   *5½*   years old!

My parents are: *Sam and Karen Johnson*

My address is: *123 Brown St.*
Somewhere, USA

My telephone number is: *(123) 555-1234*

The information in my portfolio includes:

➤ Medical information   page

➤ Educational programming (my IEP summary)   page

➤ Adaptations needed   page

➤ Communication strategies   page

➤ Reinforcement strategies   page

MEDICAL INFORMATION

My Medicines:

Susie Johnson   *May 23, 2001*

These are my medications:

Drug Name: Side Effects I Experience: Dose:

Drug Name	Why I Take It	Side Effects I Experience	Dosage	When I Take It
Tegretol	It helps to control my seizures.	Drowsiness	200 mg	At home in the morning & evening
Allegra	Hay fever	None	60 mg	Each morning before school
Flonase	Hay fever	None	One squirt in each nostril	Each night at bedtime

----

My Allergies:

I am allergic to grasses, flowers, and some types of trees. In the spring, I get really stuffed up when everything is starting to bloom.

During this time, I am more likely to have seizures. When I take my allergy medicine, I do much better.

Seizure Information

Student name: Susie Johnson   **Date:** May 25, 2002

Type of seizure I have: Generalized tonic-clonic (grand mal)

Medication: Tegretol (given at home morning and evening)

What my seizures look like: First, I stiffen and my arms and legs will extend. This lasts for less than 1 minute. Then, my body will begin to jerk. Rarely does this phase of my seizure last more than 2 minutes. (I usually wet my pants during a seizure.)

What triggers my seizures: Flickering lights
I also am more likely to have seizures when my hay fever is acting up.

Staff response: If I am sitting in my wheelchair, I will not fall out because I am strapped in very well. If I am on the floor on the mat or on the wedge, please be sure that I won't hit anything when I start to jerk. If I am positioned in my standing table, I should be ok because of how I am strapped into it. Please change my pants after a seizure. Also, I'm really tired after a seizure and will probably take a nap for about 30 minutes.

Be sure to document when my seizures occur and how long they last because my mom and dad share this information with the doctor. (There's a blank Seizure Activity Record in my portfolio for you to use.)

Program restrictions: Please avoid using flickering lights in the classroom because they sometimes trigger seizures for me.

Seizure Activity Record

Date	Time	Location	Activity	Duration	Type	Reaction	Post

Vision Information

Student name: Susie Johnson   **Date:** May 25, 2002

Vision diagnosis: I have cortical visual impairment, exotropia (my eyes tend to turn or drift to the sides because of muscle problems), and I'm extremely nearsighted (or myopic), which means it's hard for me to see things far away. I wear glasses to try to help me to see things better.

Observations: I see best when things are shown to me no more than 3 feet away.

Please see the section of the portfolio that tells about adaptations. There are lots of ideas there to help with my limited vision.

Hearing Information

Student name: Susie Johnson   **Date:** May 25, 2002

Hearing diagnosis: I've had repeated hearing tests and the results always come back inconclusive. No one seems to be quite sure how much I can hear. The doctor says that whatever my ear hears doesn't necessarily mean my brain understands the message. He calls this a Central Auditory Processing Disorder.

Medical treatment: I don't use hearing aids or have other recommendations, but there are suggestions for you in the adaptations section of my portfolio.

Restrictions and precautions: None

IEP Summary

Student: *Susie Johnson*   Date: *May 25, 2002*

School year: *2002-2003*

The following provides a <u>summary</u> (not the complete objectives) of Susie's IEP objectives:

<u>Objectives related to communication:</u>
1. *Susie will choose free time activities by picking between objects representing preferred and nonpreferred activities.*
2. *Susie will use a voice output device (e.g., BIGmack) to indicate she wants more at snack time.*
3. *Susie will use a voice output device such as the Step-by-Step Communicator to participate in morning circle.*
4. *When greeted by name, Susie will look at or turn her head toward that peer or adult.*

<u>Objectives related to: recreation activities:</u>
1. *Susie will use a switch to activate preferred toys.*
2. *Susie will extend both hands to play in materials such as finger paints.*

<u>Objectives related to other skills:</u>
1. *Susie will increase standing in a stander to 30 minutes per day during meaningful class activities.*

<u>Objectives related to reading:</u>
1. *Susie will show her preference for different types of books on tape.*

IEP Accommodations
For _Susie Johnson_

This form specifies that the following accommodations are included within the IEP for _____ Susie Johnson _____ .

1. Susie needs the following communication devices:
a. A single switch device with voice output (e.g., BIGmack)
b. A single switch device with levels with voice output (e.g., Step-by-Step Communicator)
2. Susie needs adapted toys or battery adaptors for use with a switch during free-time and other play activities
3. Susie needs a supine stander.
4. Susie needs simple children's books on tape or on computer software.
5. Susie needs the objects specified in her Communication Dictionary of this portfolio.
6. Simplify auditory and visual information.
7. Be sure things you want Susie to look at are simple and uncluttered.
8. Keep materials at a close distance.
9. Use real objects with Susie.
10. Speak to Susie in a normal tone of voice but be close to her.
11. Minimize background noise as much as possible when talking to Susie.
12. Use consistent touch, object, and other cues with Susie.

Our signatures below indicate that we have received a copy of this form and understand that these accommodations are included in the IEP.

_____   _____   _____   _____
Student Signature   Date   Special Ed. Teacher   Date

_____   _____   _____   _____
General Ed. Teacher   Date   Other   Date

Here's my Touch Cue Map:

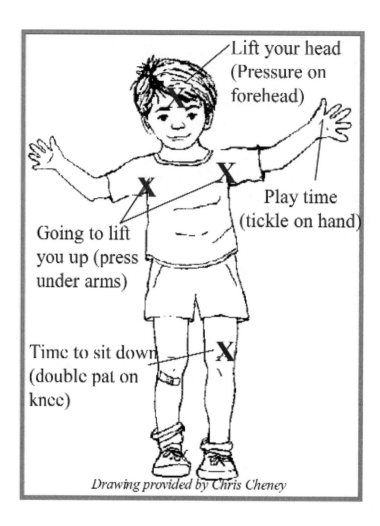

Drawing provided by Chris Cheney

COMMUNICATION DICTIONARY

Student: _Susie Johnson_   Date: _May 30, 2002_

Spoken Language:
____ Yes   _X_ ____ No   I use spoken words to communicate.

● ●

Sign Language:
____ Yes   _X_ ____ No   I use sign language to communicate.

● ●

Gestures:

I don't use any gestures right now.

● ●

Objects:

_X_ ____ Sometimes I use objects to tell others want I want. For example, I might look at or touch a cup to show someone when I want a drink. These are the objects and communicative meaning that I use as well as the activities in which I use them:

Object:	Communicative Meaning:	Activity:
Cup	_"I'm thirsty."_	_Snack & Lunch_
Spoon	_"I'm hungry."_	_Snack & Lunch_
Tape player	_"I want to listen to music."_	_Free time_
Small flashlight	_Playing with lighted toys_	_Play & free time_

● ●

PHOTOS / LINE DRAWINGS:

I don't use any photos or line drawings right now.

● ●

_X_ Yes _____ No I use a voice output device to help communicate.

The voice output device(s) I use, the symbols to be placed on the device(s), and the activities in which I use the device(s) and symbols are:

Devices (e.g., BIGmack, Step-by-Step Communicator, Alpha Talker)	Symbols (e.g., Objects, Photos, Line Drawings)	Activities (e.g., snack choices, requesting more, story time)
1. BIGmack	Objects (e.g., cup, spoon)	Snack time, lunch, free time, play
2. Step-by-Step Communicator	Objects (e.g., small bells)	Morning circle
3.		
4.		
5.		

Sometimes I use ways of communicating that are not always viewed as communication by others. However, these are sometimes the only ways I have to tell others how I feel or what I want. I probably won't use every form listed.

Form / Method:	What it means:	Activities I use it in:
_X_ Cry	_I need to change positions_	_throughout the day_
____ Aggression	_____	_____
____ Tantrum	_____	_____
____ Self-injury	_____	_____
____ Eye gaze	_____	_____
____ Pull other's hands	_____	_____
____ Touch / Move other's face	_____	_____
____ Grab / Reach	_____	_____
____ Vocalize/ Make noise	_____	_____
____ Remove self / Walk away	_____	_____
____ Facial expressions	_____	_____
____ Change in intonation	_____	_____
____ Other:	_____	_____
____ Other:	_____	_____
____ Other:	_____	_____

Reinforcement Strategies

The type of reinforcement I prefer is:

_ X _ Social   _ X _ Activities   ____Tangible objects ____ Food/Drinks
_ X _ Verbal____ Other:_____

Here is a description of reinforcing SOCIAL INTERACTIONS that work with me:

I love it when someone sits with me and rubs my shoulders or rubs lotion on my hands.

Here is a description of reinforcing ACTIVITIES that work with me:

I enjoy listening to rap music and toys with bright lights.

Here is a description of reinforcing TANGIBLE OBJECTS that work with me:

Here is a description of reinforcing FOOD/DRINKS that work with me:

VERBAL praise is most effective when delivered in this manner:

_ X _   Very enthusiastic, public praise

_____   Fairly enthusiastic, public praise

_____   Quiet, privately delivered praise

_____   Neutrally (no voice fluctuation)

Additional comments about my reinforcers:

Appendix B

Steve's Case Study

OVERVIEW

Steve is 13 years old and about to begin 7th grade at a middle school. He loves playing sports, especially soccer and basketball; he enjoys computer games and Gameboy®; and he especially enjoys Legos® and the new movie-making software that allows him to make Lego movies. Steve has mild disabilities that include a diagnosis of attention deficit disorder and learning disabilities. His specific learning disabilities are in reading and spelling as well as some difficulties with organizational skills. During the summer, his mother heard about portfolios and asked Steve to work with her to develop one for his middle school teachers since middle school was going to be a major change. Like many 13-year-olds, Steve wasn't too thrilled about working on a portfolio during his free time, but he agreed to help his mom.

They decided to include the following sections in Steve's portfolio:

1. Educational Programming (for an IEP summary)

2. Adaptations and Supports

3. Medical Information

4. Reinforcement Strategies

(It is important to note that Steve lives in a state that requires standards-based learning and has content standards for all areas of learning. Thus, all of Steve's IEP objectives are related to those content standards.)

IEP SUMMARY

Student: Steve Green   Date: *July 15, 2002*

School Year: *2002-2003*

The following provides a *summary* (not the complete objective) of
<u>*Steve's*</u> IEP objectives:

<u>Objectives related to organizational skills:</u>
1. *Begin working within 1 minute of being instructed to do so.*
2. *Work without interruption for 30 minutes.*
3. *Use a calendar system to keep track of assignments and due dates.*
4. *Record information for a research project using a self-selected note-taking or organizational strategy.*

<u>Objectives related to reading:</u>
1. *Read newspaper articles for the main idea and to be able to discuss current events.*
2. *Compare and contrast meaning of closely related words.*
3. *Demonstrate increased comprehension of written materials by showing knowledge of main plots and sub plots of stories and compare and contrast actions of characters as they relate to the plots.*
4. *Compare and contrast consumer materials such as warranties, product information, and instruction manuals.*
5. *Paraphrase and synthesize information from different sources.*

<u>Objectives related to spelling:</u>
1. *Use correct spelling of frequently used words, with special attention to roots, suffixes, and prefixes.*
2. *Spell frequently misspelled words correctly (e.g., their/they're/there and you're/your).*
3. *Use rules of capitalization.*

Assistive Technology Checklist

Student: *Steve Green*   Class: *All classes*

Communication:

____Communication board or
book (objects, line drawings,
photos)
____Simple voice output device
____Voice output device with levels
____Voice output device with
dynamic display
____Other:_____

_____

Writing:

____Adaptive pen/pencil grips
____Special pens (e.g., bold, black
pens; weighted pens, ring-pens)
____Special paper (e.g., bold lines,
raised lines)
____Writing guides (e.g., check
guide, signature guide)
____Slant board
_x_Spell checker
_x_Talking dictionary or
thesaurus
_x_Computer software:
Write Outloud

_____

____Computer keyguard
____Alternate keyboard
____Alternate mouse or track ball
____Other:_____

_____

Mathematics:

____Calculator (e.g., large keys,
voice output, print out)
____Adapted clocks & watches (e.g.,
large numbers, lighted, voice
output)
____Special measuring tools
____Talking thermometer
____Abacus
____Number line

____Computer software:

_____

_____

Reading:

____Books on tape
____Computer software:

_____

_____

Organizational and study skills:

_x_Schedules and calendars as
organizers
_x_Highlighters, highlight
tape, etc.
_x_Colored file folders to
organize materials
____Tactile materials (e.g., maps)
____Computer software:

_____

_____

Recreation activities:

____Switches
____Battery adapters
____Adapted playing cards (e.g.,
large numbers, card holder,
automatic shuffler)
____Adapted games (e.g., large
print, textures)
____Adapted balls (e.g., with
noisemakers, tactile)
____Adapted toys (e.g., handles,
textures, for use with switches)
____Computer software:

_____

_____

Checklist of Necessary Instructional, Environmental, and Material Accommodations

Student: _Steve Green_   Class: _All classes_

INSTRUCTIONAL MODIFICATIONS:

In-class instruction:

____Introduce new materials using advance organizers
____Provide an outline of the lecture
____Highlight key words or new terms
____Provide concrete examples of abstract concepts
____Provide lecture notes
_x_Allow audiotapes of lectures
_x_Allow student to copy another student's notes
_x_Provide student with copies of overhead transparencies
____Other:_____

Providing directions:

____Provide oral instructions clearly and concisely
____Repeat oral instructions
____Ask the student to repeat back instructions
____Provide instructions in writing
____Provide a demonstration of what is to be done
____Other:_____

Independent work assignments:

____Decrease number of items to be completed
____Allow all work to be completed in manuscript (i.e., no cursive)
____Allow written assignments to be completed on the computer
____Allow additional time
____Other:_____

Alternative student responses:

_x_Allow oral responses from student
____Have student tape responses
____Allow drawings instead of written responses
____Ask yes/no questions for comprehension checks
____Other:_____

Tests and evaluation of student learning:

____Provide a practice test
____Extended time
_x_Oral exams with oral responses
____Provide an alternative test (e.g., multiple choice instead of essay)
____Provide an answer list for fill-in-the blank exams
_x_Dictation of answers for essay exams
____Answer questions directly on the exam
_x_Disregard spelling and grammatical errors
____Allow use of dictionary, spell checker, or calculator
____Allow submission of alternative assignments
____Other:_____

Environmental Modifications:

_x_Preferential seating (e.g., near teacher, neat a focused student)
____Quiet area for study
_x_Study carrel for independent work

____A private location for the student to take a break
____Minimize auditory distractions
____Minimize visual distractions
____Modify lighting
____More physical space for the student to maneuver
____Other:_____

MODIFICATIONS TO MATERIALS:

Using handouts and visual aids:

____Use clear copies
____Provide copies on colored paper for some students
____Use large print
____Provide a limited amount of information per handout or visual aid
____Darken items difficult to read or see
____Other:_____

Independent work assignments:

____Intersperse practice items with new material
_x_Provide copies of textbook or workbook pages that can be written on

____Provide examples of correct responses
_x_Highlight key parts of directions
____Use color cues for starting and ending points
____Provide enough space for answers
____Allow student to supplement written answers with pictures or drawings
____Other:_____

Reading:

_x_Books on tape
____Written material paired with photos, pictures, or objects
_x_Use of highlighting tape
____Use of colored transparencies
____Other:_____

Comments:

IEP Accommodations
For _Steve Green_ .

This form specifies that the following accommodations are included within the IEP for _____ Steve Green _____ .

1. Steve carries a tape recorder with him so that he can tape lectures.

2. Please provide Steve with copies of any overhead transparencies you will be using.

3. Allow him to photocopy another student's notes.

4. Exams will be taken in the resource room where Steve will be read the tests and give oral responses that will be recorded for him.

5. Steve will complete written assignments on the computer and will use a spellchecker.

6. Please provide copies of textbook or workbook pages that can be written on so that Steve does not have to copy assignments from books.

Our signatures below indicate that we have received a copy of this form and understand that these accommodations are included in the IEP.

Steve Green	7/15/02	Karen Smith	7/15/02
Student Signature	Date	Special Ed. Teacher	Date
Jack Mason	7/15/02	Beth Green	7/15/02
General Ed. Teacher	Date	Other (Parent)	Date

Medical Information

Steve Green   *August 23, 2002*

These are my medications:

Drug Name: Side Effects I Experience: Dose:

Drug Name	Why I Take It	Side Effects I Experience	Dosage	When I Take It
Metadate ER	It helps me to focus and pay attention.	I eat very little lunch, if any.	60 mg (three 20 mg tablets)	Each morning with breakfast
Allegra	Hayfever	None	60 mg	Each morning before school
Flonase	Hayfever	None	One squirt in each nostril	Each night at bedtime

Steve Green   *August 15, 2002*

The type of reinforcement I prefer is:

____ Social   _X_ Activities   ____Tangible objects ____Food/Drinks
____ Verbal   ____ Other:_____

Here is a description of reinforcing SOCIAL INTERACTIONS that work with me:

Here is a description of reinforcing ACTIVITIES that work with me:

I love to play games on the computer during free time, especially racing games!

Here is a description of reinforcing TANGIBLE OBJECTS that work with me:

Here is a description of reinforcing FOOD/DRINKS that work with me:

I love Coca Cola and chocolate candy.

VERBAL praise is most effective when delivered in this manner:

_____ Very enthusiastic, public praise

_____ Fairly enthusiastic, public praise

_X_ Quiet, privately delivered praise

_____ Neutrally (no voice fluctuation)

Additional comments about my reinforcers:

Please don't embarrass me in front of my friends by making a big deal when I do work correctly.

Appendix C

Patrick's Case Study

OVERVIEW

Patrick is 16 years old and attends Hayward High School. Like other teenagers his age, he likes music, especially "The Cranberries," and to be with his friends. He likes animals and hopes to work with a veterinarian when he gets out of school. Patrick has many interests and talents. He also has a severe vision loss, uses a wheelchair, and needs a computer to do his schoolwork and communicate with other people. In August, the special education teacher, Mrs. Roberts, read an article about transition portfolios. She has talked to Patrick's new team and would like to develop a transition portfolio for him over the next school year. Each year, the school has new paraeducators and support personnel, and Mrs. Roberts thinks the portfolio is a great way to give information to these new people and maintain the consistency of Patrick's program. Since Patrick is new to Hayward High School, the team members determined that they would like to conduct a MAPS session for him. (His completed MAPS can be found in Chapter 3.) The team decided to begin the portfolio process by including what they currently know about him, and then collect additional information throughout the year. The sections of Patrick's portfolio will include the following:

1. Patrick's MAPS (see completed MAPS and action plan in Chapter 3)

2. Communication

3. Medical

4. Considerations for Physical Impairments

5. Educational Programming

6. Team Notes

Communication Section

General Guidelines for Communicating With Patrick

Initiation:

1. The computer should be accessible to Patrick at all times.
2. Initiation is: Anytime Patrick says something all by himself with no cue.
3. The first thing that Patrick says is initiation. Beyond the first thing, even a conversation change is turn-taking.
4. Patrick may need to be cued to learn how to initiate (e.g., "What do you think, Patrick?") The cues should be faded over time. Part of the goal is for Patrick to feel comfortable when people are silent.
5. Always reinforce Patrick's initiations. He needs to know that what he says is important.
6. If Patrick's initiation is a person's name, assume this initiation means he wants to make contact with that person.

Response

1. Response is: When Patrick is asked a question, he should give an appropriate and quick answer. He should use as many words as he can. The more, the better.

Example:

Question to Patrick: "What did you do this weekend?" If he went swimming this weekend with his brother, he might answer, "Swim," but an even better answer is "Swim Saturday" or "Swim Saturday Mike." Encourage him to use more than one word by asking who, what, when, and where questions.

<u>Guidelines on Explaining to People How to Have a
Conversation With Patrick Using</u>

<u>Yes/No Questions</u>

1. Explain that "Patrick can answer yes/no questions with his arms."
2. You then ask Patrick to "say 'Yes'" and point out his movement of both arms above his lap.
3. You then ask Patrick to "say 'No'" and point out his movement of relaxing his arms in his lap or just a slight movement of the left arm.
4. Give the person an example of a yes/no question and let Patrick answer, and then encourage the person to ask Patrick a question.

<u>Guidelines on Explaining to People and Classmates
How to Have a Conversation With</u>

<u>Patrick Using the "Budtalk Book"</u>

1. Give the person the Budtalk Book.
2. Explain to them that Patrick will tell them something and that they can then look at the corresponding photo.
3. Explain that Patrick will then ask them something.
4. Then tell Patrick to pick something to talk about.
5. Assist the person talking to Patrick by helping them with appropriate yes/no questions or cues for Patrick, and always let Patrick talk for himself.

Body Language Dictionary

Yes	Raising or moving both arms at once
No	Slight movement of left arm Relaxing both arms
Come get me	Extension of arms, legs, or torso Yells
Dislike	Body extension Moving left arm with mouth open Whining or crying, skin turns red
"Help me"	Moves arms
Bored	Stops answering questions Eyes are half closed
Like	Smiles, open-mouth vocalizations Kicking legs
More	Smile Vocalizations

Medical Section

Vision Information

Student name: Patrick Reed   **Date:** September 3, 2001

Vision diagnosis: Patrick received a functional eye exam in 1998. A summary of that report indicates that Patrick probably sees patterns and shadows. He has an asymmetrical tonic reflex to the left and his vision usually follows on that side. A Teller Acuity Test was given to Patrick and responses were seen in both eyes at about 20/150, although it was the right eye and both eyes together that appeared to be his primary strength. It was recommended that Patrick see an ophthalmologist to determine if he could wear glasses. He was seen by Dr. Green who did not feel he could benefit from glasses.

Current Status: A functional eye exam is being scheduled for late September. It is important to remember to have Patrick use his vision by pointing out things to him, the function and color, the size and shape of objects, people, and events. The functional exam will help the team determine what symbol size might be the most appropriate and how better to use his vision in daily activities.

Medication: Patrick is not currently taking any medication.

IEP SUMMARY

<u>Student</u>:   Patrick Reed   <u>Date</u>: September 5, 2001

<u>School Year</u>: 2001-2002

The following information is an overview of Patrick's program.

<u>Communication</u>:

* Patrick is currently working on greeting teachers and peers in a variety of settings across the school. His computer is programmed to initiate "Hello" and to respond "Hello" when someone greets him.

* Patrick uses his arms to answer "yes" and "no" questions. He will raise both arms above his lap for "yes" and he will relax and keep his arms in his lap or move his left arm slightly for "no."

* These are areas that Patrick can practice throughout the school day and in a variety of environments.

<u>Educational Programs</u>:

* One of Patrick's main goals is to build his vocabulary. He has daily opportunities in English, history, Spanish, and biology to learn specific words that he can use in other environments. Teachers and peers in these classes should feel comfortable in asking him questions that require him to use the words he is learning.

<u>Positioning</u>:

It is important that Patrick be positioned in certain ways during the day. He needs to get out of the wheelchair and use a classroom chair several times a day. This can be accomplished in any of his classes. He also needs to be positioned in a stander for 30 to 45 minutes a day. This can be done in drama or biology—neither has desks.

Instructional Schedule Matrix

	Greetings	Vocabulary Building	Yes/No With arms	Choice Scanning	"Who/what" Questions	"Things I Need"	"What do You Think?"	Bench/floor Sitting	Standing/Walker
English M-F	x	x	x	x	x	x	x	x	
Math M-F	x		x	x	x	x	x	x	
History M-F	x	x	x	x	x	x	x	x	
Break M-F	x							x	
Drama M-W-F	x		x	x				x	x
Office aide T-Th	x		x	x		x		x	
Lunch M-F	x					x	x	x	
Spanish M-F	x	x	x		x		x	x	
Biology M-F	x	x	x	x	x	x	x	x	x

Classroom Participation Plan

<u>Student</u>: Patrick Reed

<u>Class</u>:   Drama

<u>Basic skill objectives</u>:

1. Greeting peers/teacher   2. Choice scanning   3. Using supine stander   4. Answering "Who/What" questions

<u>Class activity</u>: Choosing parts for the school play

The drama class assignment is to get together and choose parts for a school play, which will take place in November. Patrick participates in the class and meets his objectives by first using his computer to greet the teacher and peers. The class paraprofessional and the other students help him into the supine stander, which is placed on one side of the circle where the students are sitting. Patrick's computer is programmed with the different parts in the play and he is asked to choose who he thinks would be best for each part. He also decides which part he would like to play (he chooses the doctor).

<u>Assistance</u>: Paraeducator, peers, and drama teacher

<u>Materials/equipment needed</u>: Supine stander and computer

Classroom Participation Plan

<u>Student</u>: Patrick Reed

<u>Class</u>:　Biology

<u>Basic skill objectives</u>:

1. Greetings　2. Vocabulary building　3. Yes/No　4. "Who, What" questions　5. "What do you think?"

<u>Class activity</u>: Students are to dissect a frog

Patrick uses his computer to greet his teacher and the members of his biology group. He is adding words from this lesson to the vocabulary list on his computer (e.g., frog, jar, cotton, dissect, heart, leg, eye). The students in the group are given a jar containing an expired frog. They are to remove the frog from the jar and decide as a group how to dissect it. The students decide that Patrick will act as a guide by answering a series of questions about the dissection. For example, they ask him if they should all dissect the frog or designate a member of the group to be in charge.

<u>Assistance</u>: Paraeducator needs to program computer for class activity; peers ask questions

<u>Materials</u>: Computer

Adaptations and Supports

Positioning Requirements

Position	Purpose	Equipment	Proper Use & Precautions	Time	Activities
Prone	Stretch out hip flexors Increase head control	* Floor mat or carpet * Small towel roll	Do not exceed ½ hr.	20-30 minutes	Listening to peers during break, drama
Sitting	Increase independence Alternate position Allow for maximum participation with peers Increase head/trunk control	* Floor * Chair * Couch	* Always sit behind him while doing any floor sitting (work down shoulders to waist, hips with hand support) * Remain close	20-30 minutes 3 x daily	Any classroom activity or lunch
Standing	To increase weight bearing through hips Provide upright position Aid in transfers and walking skills	* Rifton Supine Stander * Head pillow, leg strap, padding cloths * Walker * Body brace, inserts	* He should wear body brace/shoe inserts * ROM legs prior to placing in stander * Check feet at end * Watch circulation	30-45 minutes ** Never exceed 45 minutes	Drama, biology

References

Bailey, D. B. (1984). A triaxial mode of the interdisciplinary team and group process. *Exceptional Children, 5,* 17-25.

Bambara, L. M., & Knoster, T. (1998). *Designing positive behavior support plans.* Washington, DC: American Association on Mental Retardation.

Batshaw, M. (1991). *Your child has a disability.* Baltimore: Brookes.

Baumgart, D., Brown, L., Pumpian, I., Nisbet, J., Ford, A., Sweet, M., Messina, R., Schroeder, J. (1982). Principle of partial participation and individualized adaptations in education programs for severely handicapped students. *Journal of the Association for Persons With Severe Handicaps, 7*(2), 17-27.

Breath, D., DeMauro, G., & Snyder, P. (1997). Adaptive sitting for young children with mild to moderate motor challenges: Basic guidelines. *Young Exceptional Children, 1*(1), 10-16.

Brown, L. W. (1997). Seizure disorders. In M. L. Batshaw (Ed.), *Children with disabilities* (4th ed., pp. 553-593). Baltimore: Brookes.

Cox, M. (1999). Making the transition. *Early Developments, 3*(1), 4-6.

Cox, P. R., & Dykes, M. K. (2001). Effective classroom adaptations for students with visual impairments. *TEACHING Exceptional Children, 33*(6), 68-74.

Crossman, H. L. (1992). *Cortical visual impairment: Presentation, assessment, and management.* North Rocks, Australia: North Rocks Press.

Demchak, M. (1997). *Teaching students with severe disabilities in inclusive settings.* Washington, DC: American Association on Mental Retardation.

Demchak, M., & Bossert, K. W. (1996). *Assessing problem behaviors.* Washington, DC: American Association on Mental Retardation.

Demchak, M., & Elquist, M. (2001). *"Could you please tell my new teacher?" A parent/teacher guide to successful transitions.* Reno: University of Nevada, Reno; Nevada Dual Sensory Impairment Project.

Demchak, M., & Greenfield, R. G. (2000). A transition portfolio for Jeff, a student with multiple disabilities. *TEACHING Exceptional Children, 32*(6), 44-49.

Downing, J. E. (2002). *Including students with severe and multiple disabilities in typical classrooms: Practical strategies for teachers* (2nd ed.). Baltimore: Brookes.

Downing, J. E., & Demchak, M. (2002). First steps: Determining individual abilities and how best to support students. In J. E. Downing (Ed.),

Including students with severe and multiple disabilities in typical classrooms (2nd ed., pp. 37-70). Baltimore: Brookes.

Durand, V. M., Mapstone, E., & Youngblade, L. (1999). The role of communication partners. In J. E. Downing (Ed.), *Teaching communication skills to students with severe disabilities* (pp. 139-155). Baltimore: Brookes.

Falvey, M., Forest, M., Pearpoint, J., & Rosenberg, R. (1997). *All my life's a circle: Using the tools: Circles, MAPS, and PATHS.* Toronto, Ontario, Canada: Inclusion Press.

Ferguson, D. L., & Baumgart, D. (1991). Partial participation revisited. *Journal of the Association of Persons with Severe Handicaps, 16,* (4), 218-227.

Forest, M., & Lusthaus, E. (1989). Promoting educational equality for all students: Circles and maps. In S. Stainback, W. Stainback, & M. Forest (Eds.), *Educating all students in the mainstream of regular education* (pp. 43-57). Baltimore: Brookes.

Gee, K., Alwell, M., Graham, N., & Goetz, L. (1994). *Inclusive instructional design: Facilitating informed and active learning for individuals who are deaf-blind in inclusive schools.* San Francisco: California Research Institute.

Giangreco, M. F., Cloninger, C. J., Dennis, R. E., & Edelman, S. W. (1994). Problem-solving methods to facilitate inclusive education. In J. S. Thousand, R. A. Villa, & A. I. Nevin (Eds.), *Creativity and collaborative learning: A practical guide to empowering students and teachers* (pp. 321-346). Baltimore: Brookes.

Giangreco, M. F., Edelman, S. W., Nelson, C., Young, M. R., & Kiefer-O'Donnell, K. (1999). Changes in educational team membership for students who are deaf-blind in general education classes. *Journal of Visual Impairment and Blindness, 93,* 166-173.

Gumnit, R. J. (1983). *The epilepsy handbook: The practical management of seizures.* New York: Raven Press.

Individuals with Disabilities Education Act (IDEA) Amendments of 1997, PL 105-17, 20 U.S.C. 1400 et seq.

Keefe, C. H. (1995). Portfolios: Mirrors of learning. *TEACHING Exceptional Children, 27*(2), 66-67.

Konkle, D. F. (1991). Hearing impairment. In M. L. Batshaw (Ed.), *A complete sourcebook of daily and medical care: Your child has a disability* (pp. 120-138). Baltimore: Brookes.

La Paro, K. M., Pianta, R. C., & Cox, M. J. (2000). Teachers' reported transition practices for children transitioning into kindergarten and first grade. *Exceptional Children, 67,* 7-20.

Lowman, D. K. (1998). Preschoolers with complex health care needs in preschool classrooms. *Young Exceptional Children, 1*(4), 2-6.

McPherson, M., Arango, P., Fox, H., Lauver, C., McManus, M., Newacheck, P., Perrin, J. M., Shonkoff, J. P., & Strickland, B. (1998). A new definition of children with special health care needs. *Pediatrics, 102,* 137-139.

Mirenda, P., & Hunt, P. (1990, December). *Augmentative communication for persons with severe disabilities: "Low tech" strategies for beginning communicators.* Paper presented at the Association for Persons with Severe Disabilities, Chicago, IL.

National Information Center for Children and Youth with Disabilities. (2001, December). *Deafness and hearing loss* (Fact Sheet 3). Washington, DC: Author.

Newacheck, P. W., Strickland, B., Shonkoff, J. P., Perrin, J. M., McPherson, M., McManus, M., Lauver, C., Fox, H., & Arango, P. (1998). An epidemiologic profile of children with special health care needs. *Pediatrics, 102,* 117-123.

O'Brien, J., & O'Brien, C. L. (Eds.). (1998). *A little book about person-centered planning.* Toronto, Ontario, Canada: Inclusion Press.

O'Neill, R. E., Horner, R. H., Albin, R. W., Sprague, J. R., Storey, K., & Newton, J. S. (1997). *Functional assessment and program development for problem behavior: A practical handbook* (2nd ed.). Pacific Grove, CA: Brooks/Cole.

Parnes, S. J. (1981). *The magic of your mind.* Buffalo, NY: Creative Education Foundation Inc., in association with Bearly Limited.

Parnes, S. J. (1992). *Source book for creative problem-solving: A fifty year digest of proven innovation processes.* Buffalo, NY: Creative Education Foundation Press.

Rainforth, B., & York-Barr, J. (1996). Handling and positioning. In F. P. Orelove & D. Sobsey (Eds.), *Educating children with multiple impairments: A transdisciplinary approach* (3rd ed., pp. 79-118). Baltimore: Brookes.

Romer, L. T., & Byrne, A. R. (1995). Collaborative teaming to support participation in inclusive education settings. In N. G. Haring & L. T. Romer (Eds.), *Welcoming students who are deaf-blind into typical classrooms* (pp. 143-169). Baltimore: Brookes.

Rous, B., & Hallam, R. A. (1998). Easing the transition to kindergarten: Assessment of social, behavioral, and functional skills in young children with disabilities. *Young Exceptional Children, 1*(4), 17-26.

Salend, S. (1998). Using portfolios to assess student performance. *TEACHING Exceptional Children, 31*(2), 36-43.

Sobsey, D., & Cox, A. (1996). Integrating health care and educational programs. In F. P. Orelove & D. Sobsey (Eds.), *Educating children with multiple disabilities* (3rd ed., pp. 217-251). Baltimore: Brookes.

Sobsey, D., & Thuppal, M. (1996). Children with special health care needs. In F. P. Orelove & D. Sobsey (Eds.), *Educating children with multiple disabilities* (3rd ed., pp. 161-216). Baltimore: Brookes.

Thousand, J. S., & Villa, R. A. (1992). Collaborative teams: A powerful tool in school restructuring. In R. A. Villa, J. S. Thousand, W. Stainback, & S. Stainback (Eds.), *Restructuring for caring and effective education* (pp. 73-108). Baltimore: Brookes.

U. S. Department of Education. (2000). *Digest of educational statistics, chapter 2. Elementary and secondary education.* Retrieved January 4, 2001, from http://nces.ed.gov/pubs2001/digest/

Index

**CORWIN
PRESS**

The Corwin Press logo—a raven striding across an open book—represents the happy union of courage and learning. We are a professional-level publisher of books and journals for K-12 educators, and we are committed to creating and providing resources that embody these qualities. Corwin's motto is "Success for All Learners."